# THE GOD PROBLEM

## ALTERNATIVES TO FUNDAMENTALISM

**Thomas A. Burch**
Bremerton, WA

Westar Institute

# THE GOD PROBLEM

## ALTERNATIVES TO FUNDAMENTALISM

### NIGEL LEAVES

POLEBRIDGE PRESS

Cover and interior design by Robaire Ream
Cover illustration by Robaire Ream

**Library of Congress Cataloging-in-Publication Data**

Leaves, Nigel, 1958-
   The God problem : alternatives to fundamentalism / Nigel Leaves.
      p. cm.
   Includes bibliographical references and index.
   ISBN-13: 978-0-944344-98-9 (alk. paper)
   1. God. 2. Spirituality. I. Title.
   BL473.L435 2006
   211--dc22

                                                   2006025240

For Sebastian

# Contents

# PREFACE

In his latest book, *Looking in the Distance*, Richard Holloway describes his journey out of organized religion and into the company of those fellow seekers who are trying to discover spiritual meaning in themselves, the extended human family, and the cosmos they inhabit. Having spent most of his life as an official representative of the Christian Church, Holloway now counts himself amongst those whose spirituality is no longer grounded in a particular religion or even a sense of God. It is an all-too familiar story, one rooted in the decline of traditional Christianity and the corresponding rise of what has been termed "the spiritual search." The thesis of this book is that the major factor in the waning of Christian faith is its continuing insistence on a supernatural God—the Almighty, the lawgiver and judge who "convicts the world of sin." A significant number of people no longer find propositional Christianity attractive. Many are creating new ways of understanding and relating to "God" in an attempt to make sense of their lives, the world, and the nagging notion of something greater that has created and sustains it all.

This book is something of a departure from my two previous works that analyzed the religious outlook of Don Cupitt (*Odyssey on the Sea of Faith* and *Surfing on the Sea of Faith*). And yet, as the saying goes, *plus ça change, plus c'est la même chose*, for in a very real sense this volume continues Cupitt's life-long theological quest for meaningful ways to speak about "God" today. To that end, I will evaluate four ways of addressing the "God problem"—panentheism, non-realism, grassroots spirituality, and religious naturalism. These are the most current responses to the increasing difficulty of God-talk in the context of both the resurgence of religious fundamentalism and the latest critical and scientific thinking. Indeed, this book might well serve in a church or university setting as both a point of departure and a resource for a discussion on how we may speak of God today.

My thanks go out to Tom Hall for his friendship and skilful editing. I am also indebted to Char Matejovsky at Polebridge Press; and the late Robert Funk, without whose challenge to turn Westar lectures into a form available to the general reader this book would not have been written. All of us are the wiser for having met "Bob" and much the poorer for his passing. And special thanks are due my wife Julie, who has once again supported my endeavors and even encouraged her husband to travel the world in pursuit of the necessary religious dialogue at conferences.

I dedicate this book to Sebastian, my ten-year-old son and golfing prodigy. Since I began *Odyssey* and *Surfing*, he has been accustomed to seeing his dad wrestle over countless drafts of chapters—all the time wondering what on earth I was doing. His gleeful laughter as he leans over the back of my chair to investigate what is on my computer screen has been all the incentive needed to continue this project. More important, I hope that this book will give him some clues as to the options for his own spiritual journey.

Nigel Leaves
John Wollaston Theological College
Perth, Western Australia

# INTRODUCTION

This book began as a series of lectures entitled "The God Problem" that the late Robert W. "Bob" Funk invited me to deliver at the Westar Institute's Spring 2005 meeting in Santa Rosa, California. It was an honor to have been associated, albeit too briefly, with this brave Christian pioneer, a visionary committed to removing theological barriers in the pursuit of the "Fourth R"—religious literacy. Funk was concerned that Christian academics had for too long concealed the results of their biblical, historical, and theological research by confining their discussions to their scholarly colleagues and by employing an obscure, specialized style of discourse. Thus theological debate was often hidden from ordinary folk; and church-goers were fed a theological diet that was not only out-of-date, but inappropriate for living in postmodernity. Worst of all, it was dishonest to the founder of their faith.[1] Funk insisted that religious scholars should conduct their deliberations in public and report the results to a broad audience in simple, non-technical language. To this end, after many years in academia, he founded the nonprofit Westar Institute in Santa Rosa in 1985 to promote research and education in biblical literacy. Westar Institute's *First Agenda*, the Jesus Seminar, was a renewed quest for the historical Jesus.

Funk's *First Agenda* was to gather a group of scholars to investigate the historical authenticity of the reported sayings of Jesus, and to assess the validity of those reports by voting on them with red, pink, grey, and black colored beads. The goal was to separate historical fact from theological fictions in the writings of the first Christians. At the same time, the definition of the New Testament was expanded to include such very early writings as the Saying Source (Q) and the Gospel of Thomas. The Jesus Seminar's detailed investigations sought to distinguish the historical Jesus from the Christ(s) proclaimed by the early Christian churches. The historical Jesus of Nazareth who emerged from the Seminar's years of scholarly research was sharply at odds with the divine figure preached by the Church. The "official" mythical matrix put forward by the Church and enshrined in its Creeds—Son of God, miracle worker, atoning savior, and apocalyptic prophet—was replaced by the Jesus Seminar's portrait of an itinerant wisdom teacher who proclaimed the reign of unconditional love.[2] In true Biblical fashion, the results of this research were "proclaimed from the hilltops," with Funk using the media to promote this new understanding of Jesus. Television interviews and news-paper reports fuelled the debate that arose from the Seminar's depiction of Jesus as one of the great sages of history rather than the divine savior derived from an uncritical reading of the New Testament.

Funk also encouraged Westar to extend its program from investigating the historical veracity of the Gospels to dealing with questions of theology. Thus a transition to a *Second Agenda* occurred in the period between 1999 and 2001. The radical findings of the Jesus Seminar had clearly challenged the faith that the Christian Church had handed on for centuries. How would this new understanding of Jesus be received by the churches? Indeed, could this Jesus be accommodated by *any* of the contemporary churches? What was the faith of the future going to look like if this new portrait of Jesus was acknowledged by Christian ministers and laity?[3]

Funk outlines three issues related to this *Second Agenda*.[4] First he asks whether the supernatural overlay of the Gospel story can still survive as myth. If, for instance, we follow the German theologian Rudolf Bultmann's call to "demythologize," we assert that the mythical, supernatural framework of angels, demons, virgin birth, resurrection etc. no longer works for us. But can the myth still make sense as myth *or* do we need to invent a new story "more compatible with modern sensibilities?" In *Christianity Rediscovered* Vincent Donovan offers a striking illustration of how inappropriate religious myths are in a different cultural setting. When Donovan, a Catholic priest, was assigned to a Catholic mission in Loliondo in East Africa, he noticed that the members of the neighboring Masai tribe remained resistant to the Christian message. Donovan wrote to his Bishop asking permission to try a novel approach to evangelism. His proposal was that since the Christian message had value for people, rather than expect the Masai to come to him, he would go and live amongst them. He soon discovered how counterpro-ductive biblical myth could be as a means of communicating Christianity to those of another culture:

> [An] assumption on which missionary work was built was this: we had to convince the world of sin . . . or the world would never feel the need for redemption, and the Redeemer. We had to tell them of the sin of Adam, original sin, which we all inherited, or the world would never feel any need for Christ. . . . Having no other tradition to rely on, I did just that with the Masai—the story of Adam and Eve and the garden and the fruit tree, and the serpent and the Fall. The trouble was that they had their own stories about the beginning of the human race. . . . In no way do any of the[ir] stories bring about a consciousness of guilt, or need for personal redemption, any more, I suspect, than the story of Adam succeeds in doing for the young people of our culture today. The Masai complained, with some justification, that our story about the beginning of the human race is more than a bit agriculturally biased, what with the garden and the fruit trees and the command to till the soil. For

them, the cowboys of East Africa, tilling the soil is anathema. Only an *olmeg* (a farmer, a barbarian) would cut open the thin layer of topsoil nurturing the life-giving grass of the Masai steppes, exposing it to the merciless equatorial sun, and turning it into desert within years. So, understandably, all their stories of the human race are veterinary in character, that is they all refer to cattle raising in some way. The story of the garden of Eden was bad enough. I followed with a worse one, the story of the first farmer, Cain, murdering the first cattlemen, Abel—the beginning, as the Masai saw it even by our accounting, of the troubles between the two groups even until now. And Cain got away with it, just as the farmers do today, and always have, with the government backing them. They began to wonder if that book I held in my hands with such great reverence was not some kind of an agricultural or governmental plot against them. And after hearing their myths and stories, it seemed a little strange offering ours about a man and a woman in the garden of Eden, and a fruit tree with forbidden fruit, as the definitive and final story about the origin of evil in the world, pretending our story were not a myth, a myth with a very important teaching perhaps, but a myth nonetheless, and one encased in a very pronounced cultural setting at that. I never told the story again.[5]

The key words here are the final ones. *I never told the story again.* The myth had no currency and therefore had to be discarded. In a similar vein Funk urges us to ask which of the myths in our Christian story no longer hold currency for us. Is the Bible's supernatural content still appropriate today?

Allied to this is the second issue of whether our foundational myths can be attributed to the creative powers of their originators. To put it starkly, is the Christian story exclusively a product of the human imagination? If so, how do we retell that story in a way that has meaning for people in the Third Millennium? To paraphrase the Psalmist, "How can we sing the Lord's song in postmodernity?" Roy Hoover gives a concrete illustration of the problem in his "Incredible Creed, Credible Faith." After Church one Sunday a long-time parishioner challenges him: "Why is it that when so much has changed in the way that we understand ourselves and the world that the Church insists on clinging to its old traditional language of faith?" Hoover suggests two reasons. For one thing, the traditional language offers a sense of connection with the past—it reminds us that we are part of an historical tradition that is in continuity with the Church of ancient times. For another, churches fear alienating or even losing some parishioners by altering the familiar message The parishioner responds, "Yes, and no one believes it anymore."[6] In short, people have moved on in their thinking and the Church is mired in the thought-forms of a forgotten age.

Funk's third issue, the contrast between the mythical portrait and the historical Jesus, is clearly beyond the scope of this volume. I will content myself with dealing with the first two issues by examining the work of three Westar Institute Fellows who have had a defining influence on the *Second Agenda*—

John Shelby Spong, Don Cupitt, and Lloyd Geering. All three acknowledge that the God of the old theism has died and ponder what kind of Christianity emerges when its supernatural underpinning is questioned or debated. The crucial problem that arises is this: if Christianity is a human creation, is God a human creation as well? And if so, what is left for people to believe in? Or, to reformulate the title of this book, what are the options for Christianity when God becomes a problem?

Insofar as these questions relate to the Jesus of history vs. the Christ of faith, the debate is best left to other Fellows of the Jesus Seminar. Indeed, they have already begun to address that problem and even suggested provisional answers. *Profiles of Jesus* (Polebridge, 2002) presents a number of essays on the historical Galilean teacher, and the aptly titled volume *The Historical Jesus Goes to Church* (Polebridge, 2004) paves the way for realigning the historical research with what is proclaimed in Churches on a Sunday morning.

Thus what has emerged from Westar research and has resulted in the *Second Agenda* is a two-pronged reassessment of the very foundations of Christianity. First, if Jesus is not the Divine Second Person of the Trinity but a wandering sage whose message was one of radical inclusivity and who preached about a kingdom of justice and peace, then how do we interpret traditional Christian doctrines such as the incarnation? Still more fundamental—and the main subject of this book—is this question: Is it still possible to use the word "God" in a meaningful sense? For example, is it reasonable to believe in the notion of a God involved in the very fabric of creation and the events of history in the wake of the Hurricane Katrina or the recent deaths of a thousand Muslim pilgrims? Is it not more reasonable, as Sam Harris argues, to wonder whether there is a God at all?

> Consider the destruction that Hurricane Katrina leveled on New Orleans. More than a thousand people died, tens of thousands lost all their earthly possessions, and nearly a million were displaced. It is safe to say that almost every person living in New Orleans at the moment Katrina struck believed in an omnipotent, omniscient and compassionate God. But what was God doing while a hurricane laid waste to their city? Surely he heard the prayers of those elderly men and women who fled the rising waters for the safety of their attics, only to be slowly drowned there. These were people of faith. These were good men and women who had prayed throughout their lives. Only the atheist has the courage to admit the obvious: these poor people died talking to an imaginary friend. Of course, there had been ample warning that a storm "of biblical proportions" would strike New Orleans, and the human response to the ensuing disaster was tragically inept. But it was inept only by the light of science. Advance warning of Katrina's path was wrested from mute Nature by meteorological calculations and satellite imagery. God told no one of his plans. Had the residents of New Orleans been content to rely on the beneficence of

the Lord, they wouldn't have known that a killer hurricane was bearing down upon them until they felt the first gusts of wind on their faces. Nevertheless, a poll conducted by *The Washington Post* found that 80% of Katrina's survivors claim that the event has only strengthened their faith in God. As Hurricane Katrina was devouring New Orleans, nearly a thousand Shiite pilgrims were trampled to death on a bridge in Iraq. There can be no doubt that these pilgrims believed mightily in the God of the Koran: their lives were organized around the indisputable fact of his existence; their women walked veiled before him; their men regularly murdered one another over rival interpretations of his word. It would be remarkable if a single survivor of this tragedy lost his faith. More likely, the survivors imagine that they were spared through God's grace.[7]

These two attacks on traditional religious belief are, as Funk explains, inextricably linked:

> Christian theologians have traditionally held that Jesus is God. If Jesus is not God, or at least the son of God, we will have to revise our notions of God. However, the old concept of God has suffered erosion in and of itself. We can no longer understand God as the creator of the species. We can no longer understand God as an interventionist tyrant as he is depicted in the Old Testament. . . . God has become mostly unemployed as the old doctrines have atrophied. At the same time, our notions of the physical universe have left God homeless. . . . The problem we face is that God is not a primary datum. An experience of God, or a revelation from God, is an interpreted experience, since there is no such thing as an uninterpreted experience. It seems we have invented God in our own image.[8]

Funk sees that a crisis point has been reached: both the existence of God and how we might best understand that word must be rigorously debated. There can be no escape or retreat into traditional thinking. The results of the search for the historical Jesus have thrown into question the Church's established theological claims about him. Moreover, traditional beliefs about God cannot be sustained in the light of the latest scientific and critical thinking. What can be done? What does "God" mean in the twenty-first century?

### PANENTHEISM

In this book I will examine four ways of resolving this theological crisis. The first approach, termed panentheism, is effectively illustrated in the books of Bishop John Shelby Spong. Panentheism (from the Greek "everything in God") rejects the traditional supernatural theism that imagines God in personal terms and posits a Deity beyond nature who at times directly intervenes in the lives of believers and unbelievers, as well as natural events. Panentheists see God more as an all-encompassing Spirit, not separate from the world, but surpassing the world we know—a presence within us and yet beyond our everyday lives. Panentheists are content not to understand fully that which they view as a sacred Mystery that somehow both sustains and transcends the Universe. Since this theological position—generally associated with "liberal Christianity"—has wide-ranging implications for Christian doctrine, I will explore how Spong understands Jesus, the Church, evangelism, and prayer.

## NON-REALISM

The second way is perhaps more controversial. Commonly labeled "non-realism," it characterizes the recent work of Don Cupitt and Lloyd Geering. Cupitt and Geering wrote independently of each other and on opposite sides of the world (England and New Zealand), yet in 1980 came to the same dramatic conclusion that the word "God" should be stripped of its supernatural content. They were both indebted to the philosopher Immanuel Kant, who had argued that we can construct a theory of knowledge without any recourse to a Divine Being as guarantor of objectivity. Having created language and thereby the world it mediated to them, human beings could make perfectly good sense of their world without any help from "above." Therefore, they agreed, people must get over the realist idea of an actual personal being who created and still sustains the Universe. The word "God" need not be abandoned, however, for it remains a potentially useful metaphor pointing to a spiritual ideal. To employ the word "God" was not to talk about a metaphysical Being, but to assist people to live *religiously*. Such a life might blend the ethics of Christianity with the spirituality of Buddhism, and could be described as reflecting a kind of "godless morality." Christian doctrines are to be understood in existential terms: for example, to believe in God as Creator is to understand one's existence as pure and gracious gift. Cupitt and Geering do not nullify Christian doctrines, but much as the philosopher Ludwig Wittgenstein advised, translate them into rules of life. Their non-realism is often referred to as "radical Christianity."

## SPIRITUALITY REVOLUTION

A third solution is one not addressed by Funk. Indeed, most people assume that especially in America the battle-lines are drawn between Christian liberalism and fundamentalism. I will argue, however, that the rivalry among Christians in what was once Christendom is only part of a larger picture of religious/spiritual searching that has been labeled: "the spirituality revolution."

Although I live in a country that has been described as the most non-religious nation on earth (New Zealand and Australia carry on an Antipodean rivalry as to who is more secular), yet even here I am aware of a proliferation of religious options. A widespread rejection of Christianity has given rise to what has been labelled "grassroots spirituality"—a movement that, if the research is correct, may in the future claim far more adherents than the organized religions. This "spirituality revolution" is being fuelled by ordinary folk who are moving away from the historic religions and forging a multitude of spiritual paths. What I will call a "smorgasbord of therapeutic spiritualities" is now available for people to pick and choose from, and many find no need to cross the threshold of a church.

### RELIGIOUS NATURALISM

The fourth solution I shall examine, religious naturalism, is allied to non-realism and grows especially out of the writings of Geering. Rejecting the idea of an objective deity, religious naturalists use the word "God" to encourage people to view the earth as sacred. The biologist Ursula Goodenough neatly explains religious naturalists and their use of "God":

> There are two flavors of God people: those whose God is natural and those whose God is supernatural. Certainly there are a lot of people within religious naturalism who have no problem with God language—God as love, God as evolution, God as process. People see God as part of nature and give God-attributes to the part of nature they find most sacred. I encounter people like that all of the time.[9]

The planet, its history and the evolutionary story must be maintained because they are sacred and are the object of devotion. While lacking any notion of a Being who watches over the actions of humans, religious naturalists have a deep spiritual concern for the earth's fragile ecosystem and the cosmos they are part of. Even if one does not believe in God, awe and wonder are appropriate responses; and religious naturalists like Geering join forces with ecologists in arguing for a moral imperative: that in a world seemingly hell-bent on self-destruction, this earth and its creatures be respected and cherished.

In short, I will seek throughout this book to widen the scope of what is deemed Christianity, to investigate the spirituality revolution in our midst, and to suggest how we might respond. I will attempt to show that the populist spirituality revolution of the new millennium challenges both liberalism *and* fundamentalism, for it represents not an either/or situation, but the increasingly diverse religious landscape that we inhabit.

This reflects, after all, the Jesus Seminar's new agenda—the future faith—and it goes to Robert Funk's central issue: the supernatural overlay of the Christian story. In a nutshell, it is the problem of God: how can we today believe in or even talk about God in a meaningful way? What kind of Christianity emerges once you start to tinker with ideas of God? Does the

Christian story depend on belief in someone/something greater than us, or can it be reformed or restructured by new understandings of who/what God is? Will Christianity survive, and if so, what will it look like?

But first, let us examine the religious situation as it appears in the first decade of this new millennium. The ascendancy of the religious right and the spread of fundamentalism have greatly altered the religious landscape of the world, with fear and *terror* now associated with being religious . . .

# 1

## SETTING THE SCENE
## THE TERROR OF GOD

Monotheists (who include most Jews, Christians, and Muslims) may worship the same single, transcendental deity, whether known by the name of Jehova [sic], the Trinity or Allah ('the God' as Muslims know Him). But when it comes to understanding His will, or intentions, His self-proclaimed followers invariably adopt opposing standpoints. For the secular non-believer, or for the liberal believer who takes a sophisticated view of religious discourse, the god of fundamentalism must be mischievous, if not downright evil, a demonic power who delights in setting humans at each other's throats.[1]

### IT IS A FACT: GOD HAS BECOME A PROBLEM!

The early twenty-first century has witnessed a dangerous shift in focus about belief (or non-belief) in God. The nineteenth and twentieth century disputation about God was a cerebral affair conducted by philosophers and theologians. Atheists such as Friedrich Nietzsche, Antony Flew and Bertrand Russell argued the case against God's existence whilst guardians of the Christian faith like Karl Barth, Clive Staples Lewis and Richard Swinburne reiterated that God was all too real.[2] The competing armies waged war with pen and ink, for the most part from the ivory towers of academia. There were no imposed *fatwas*, no assassination threats, no burning of homes or suicide bombers. As products of the Enlightenment, the combatants were reasoning and reasonable people, and once they had stated their arguments and "let off steam" they were content to allow God (if She existed) to settle the argument *after* the death of the contestants.

To be sure, the debate about God had often exhibited a more sinister aspect. The history of the Church is littered with despicable deeds of barbarity perpetrated by Christians against other Christians lest mortal souls be eternally lost because of "false teaching." And even in the last hundred or so years accusations of "heresy" against Christian clergy and theologians of all denominations have resulted in some of them being "silenced" either by being forbidden to write or by being forced to relinquish their employment. These have included David Strauss (Lutheran, 1831), Charles Voysey (Anglican, 1871), George Tyrell (Roman Catholic, 1907) James Chapple (Presbyterian 1910), John Dietrich (Reformed, 1911), Walter Gill (Methodist, 1964), Peter Cameron (Presbyterian, 1992), Dr. Molly Marshall (Southern Baptist, 1994),

Anthony Freeman (Anglican, 1994) Tissa Balasuriya (Roman Catholic, 1996), Michael Marwood (Roman Catholic, 1998), and Andrew Furlong (Anglican, 2001). Whilst these individuals no doubt felt they had been subjected to "mental torture" and had experienced the effects of "the modern inquisition" there were no physically violent deeds perpetrated by the "god-fearing" against the "godless."[3] This is not always the case today, where religions, once aptly described as "licensed insanities," have sometimes run amok:

> Religion is as much a living spring of violence today as it was at any time in the past. The recent conflicts in Palestine (Jews versus Muslims), the Balkans (Orthodox Serbians versus Catholic Croatians; Orthodox Serbians versus Bosnian and Albanian Muslims), Northern Ireland (Protestants versus Catholics), Kashmir (Muslims versus Hindus), Sudan (Muslims versus Christians and animists), Nigeria (Muslims versus Christians), Ethiopia and Eritrea (Muslims versus Christians), Sri Lanka (Sinhalese Buddhists versus Tamil Hindus), Indonesia (Muslims versus Timorese Christians), Iran and Iraq (Shiite versus Sunni Muslims), and the Caucasus (Orthodox Russians versus Chechen Muslims; Muslim Azerbaijanis versus Catholic and Orthodox Armenians) are merely a few cases in point. In these places religion has been the explicit cause of literally millions of deaths in the last ten years.[4]

Indeed, the stakes have been raised to a new and frightening level. Medieval attitudes have returned. Rational argument and scholarly discussion have been replaced by intolerance and a level of hatred that has led to physical threats and brutal acts of violence. I had an inkling of this myself as far back as 1978. During the University vacation, together with five fellow students and a college professor, I visited some of the more remote regions of northeast Turkey and even crossed over into Iran, where we miraculously escaped being caught up in the dramatic events incident to the toppling of the last Shah of Persia. Unwittingly, we had timed our trip to coincide with the Islamic festival of Ramadan and were often faced with the daunting prospect of trying to find food for lunch with no shops open until early evening. One particularly hot and dusty day in a secluded location not far from Mount Ararat, having run out of provisions, we were looking for a friendly shopkeeper when we approached a boy, probably about twelve years of age, and asked for directions. He replied in broken English wanting to know whether we were Christians. When we acknowledged that we were, he made the sign of the cross with two fingers and then proceeded to spit on them. He ran off uttering what we could only imagine were hostile threats. Whilst we dismissed the incident at the time as just an isolated case of childish ignorance, the events of the last few years have reawakened memories of that unpleasant episode and jolted me out of my comfortable lethargy to ask some obvious but important questions. What was it in that boy's religious upbringing that had instilled in him such hatred of another person's religious conviction?

Was his an isolated case, or did his whole neighborhood, town or city believe the same thing? How could religion inspire such intolerance? How long ago had the seeds of distrust been sown? Had he now a quarter of a century later joined a Muslim extremist group?

Of course my initial encounter with another religious tradition should not have been such a huge surprise. The same sort of hostility—formerly aroused by co-religionists one considered heretical—had been alive for generations within Christianity not more than a hundred miles across the Irish Sea from my hometown. Anyone growing up in the United Kingdom in the 1970s and '80s was conscious of a sectarian religious war being waged by those allegedly belonging to the *same* religion. Nightly our television news showed scenes of wanton destruction of both property and people by bombs indiscriminately planted by the Irish Republican Army with strong links to the Roman Catholic Church; daily we saw images of such firebrand preachers as the ultra-Protestant Reverend Ian Paisley calling on heaven to smite Roman Catholics. Surely all this should have stamped vividly upon my consciousness the recognition that religious people were not always loving or rational. Of course, some might object that this bloody conflict was not intrinsically religious, but was rooted in the resurgence of Irish nationalism in opposition to British rule, and hence essentially political. I would reply that this interpretation ignores the palpable presence of religious identity (Catholic versus Protestant) that divides Northern Ireland. I would urge skeptics to visit either the Falls Road or the Shankill Road in Belfast and read the murals of hate directed at those of another denomination. There you will see the motto for the Ulster Volunteer Force: "For GOD and ULSTER." In like manner those who champion the Republican movement often paint a Celtic cross next to an armed resistance fighter. Moreover, both sides conduct traditional annual marches to commemorate Protestant and Catholic victories of the past. Religion and politics are inextricably intertwined. Few (if any) Irish Protestants would support the Irish Republican Army, and few (if any) Irish Catholics would support the Ulster Volunteer Force. As Malise Ruthven insightfully comments,

> Irish Catholicism . . . has developed into a nationalist ideology in which religion has become a marker of communal identity.[5]

This is poignantly described by Frank McCourt in his autobiography, *Angela's Ashes*, as the Catholic Church and Irish nationalism combine to instill a sense of martyrdom in its youth:

> The master says it's time to prepare for First Confession and First Communion, to know and remember all the question and answers in the catechism, to become good Catholics, to know the difference between right and wrong, to die for the Faith if called on. The master says it's a glorious thing to die for

the Faith and Dad says it's a glorious thing to die for Ireland and **I wonder if there's anyone in the world who would like us to live**.[6]

Sad to say, that "battle for God" has intensified in recent years to include anyone from the secular world who dared question or oppose someone's religious point of view.[7] From the Christian cry of "whoever is not with me is against me" (Matthew 13:30) to the Islamic citation from the Koran, "the infidels will never stop fighting us until we follow their way," the war-cry of the fundamentalist has become more belligerent. It is indisputable that the enemy has now become *personal*. Not only individuals like Salman Rushdie, but such groups as religious writers, artists, cartoonists, film-makers, abortion doctors, and gay and lesbian communities have felt the wrath of extremists whose God needs protecting against the evil ways of those they despise.[8] The existence of God has become more than an intellectual question. God must not be debated, but *defended* at all costs against the infidel and unbeliever.

Of course, these include not only those who question or deny the existence of God, but those whose interpretation of God differs from one's own or who dare to derogate one's holy book. Indeed, for many of the so-called "people of the book"—Christians, Muslims and Jews—God and their holy book are synonymous. They will not permit their scriptures to be subjected to the same protocols of historical and literary criticism that are used to analyze every other piece of literature. This is sacred writing—the Word of God—which has been dictated unblemished and without error. It is as if God literally uttered actual human words to a consortium of ancient stenographers who needed no correcting fluid nor ever resorted to the erase button on their machines! To question the revelation of God as set out in his holy book is tantamount to blasphemy—a sin for which that inerrant text prescribes death as a mandatory punishment.

What I have just written is neither fanciful thinking nor scaremongering. In 2004 Theo van Gogh, a provocateur and *enfant terrible* of the Dutch cinema, was ambushed and killed by a bearded man in Arab clothing as he cycled through the heart of Amsterdam. The man was later identified as Mohammed Bouyeri, a Muslim of Dutch-Moroccan nationality, and his attack was prompted by the director's film, *Submission*, which highlights the repression of women in some Islamic cultures. Part of his footage depicted a voluptuous girl in a transparent gown with verses of the Koran painted across her naked chest, back, stomach and thighs—ostensibly to dramatize the humanity of the oppressed female beneath the Muslim veil. The film was scripted by Ayaan Hirsi Ali, a Somali refugee and feminist convert, who denounces Islam as a medieval, misogynist cult that is at odds with the modern world. She escaped to the Netherlands in 1992 to avoid an arranged marriage. At age five she had undergone the ordeal of female genital mutilation, a custom still practiced in many Muslim communities. This and other grievances against Islamic practice lead her to reject her faith and seek to aid other women oppressed by outmoded traditions. Despite the threat to her own life, Ms. Hirsi Ali refuses to back down on what she calls her Islam Reform Project (IRP): "I am on a mission. And it has only just begun." She has been subjected to several *fatwas* or death threats, and requires round-the-clock protection. Mohammed Bouyeri was convicted on July 26th, 2005, and sentenced to life in prison without parole.

"Multiculturalism" and "pluralism," the buzz-words of tolerance, have been replaced by absolutes: "fundamentalism" and "true believers." In an increasingly globalized world where religions cannot ignore each other—because they daily rub shoulders and compete with each other—to deny pluralism is to light the fuse for bloody confrontation. And yet for the devout followers of most religions, to openly acknowledge the pluralist paradigm that there are many ways to the Holy would mean that Truth is compromised, and so is God! For the fundamentalist, the Enlightenment project that champions pluralism as well as new freedoms of speech, action, and thought must be rejected. Religious ideology must replace it, hastening our return to

> the divine right of kings, feudalism, the caste system, slavery, political executions, forced castration, vivisection, bearbaiting, honorable duels, chastity belts, trial by ordeal, child labor, human and animal sacrifice, the stoning of heretics, cannibalism, sodomy laws, taboos against contraception, human radiation experiments—the list is nearly endless.[9]

Such a trend can be seen not only in the Islamic world, but in the heartland of Western progressivism. The growing conservatism of Christian churches has set off alarm bells. In 2005 liberal Christians greeted with trepidation the election of Cardinal Ratzinger (the former head of the Congregation for the Doctrine of Faith, in earlier times known as the Inquisition) as Pope Benedict XVI. His recent condemnation of divorce, artificial birth control, and trial and gay marriages has reinforced the widespread notion that religion is opposed to human freedom and sexual expression. Consider for example the issue of homosexuality.

It is encouraging to note that the late Cardinal Basil Hume, the former Roman Catholic Archbishop of Westminster, was privately in favor of gay rights.[10] Yet it is unfortunate that like many who hold public office within the Church, he saw himself as a "man under authority" and toed the party line for the sake of the alleged "unity of the Church." A similarly schizoid stance has been adopted by the Anglican Archbishop of Canterbury, Rowan Williams. Prior to his enthronement as head of the Anglican Communion, he had argued that there was no theological reason why ordained homosexuals should not hold the office of Bishop. In 2004, however, in view of his new position and in response to pressure from the conservative wing of the Church, he barred the consecration of the Reverend Canon Jeffrey John (an openly gay priest living in a long-term relationship with another man) as Bishop of Reading.

How have we arrived at this perilous state of affairs? More important, can we extricate ourselves from it? A recent spate of books on the terror of fundamentalism and its dire consequences has predicted that Armageddon might not be too far off.[11] The nuclear apocalypticism of the 1970s and '80s, with the "end-game" being fought between the Soviets and the Americans, has been replaced by the clash of civilizations that is often touted as "Islam versus Christianity." This situation is exacerbated when Christian and Muslim leaders announce that God is on *their* side. Thus, the popular Christian evangelist Billy Graham thanked God for having caused the election of the American President, the President himself believed that (the Christian) God had told him to fight terrorists in Afghanistan and invade Iraq; and the Iranian President, Mahmoud Ahmadinejad, declared that his government must prepare for the Hidden Imam, the messianic figure of Shi'ite Islam.[12] Apocalyptic rhetoric by both Christian and Muslim leaders that glorifies cosmic chaos, war and bloodshed and that urges ordinary mortals to hasten the End Times, does nothing to promote world peace and stability. It is clear that the stakes have been raised to an extraordinary level.

In 1985 the popular singer Sting might have been comforted by the fact that "the Russians love their children too" (and therefore would not readily press the nuclear button to destroy themselves along with others), but the same reasoning does not apply to the suicide bomber today.[13] The Muslim martyr has no qualms about leaving this life, for paradise beckons. Furthermore, his family will rejoice at his participation in the holy "struggle" (*jihad*) and will be granted God's blessing for his holy sacrifice.[14] Whether the martyr's rewards will match his expectations is a matter of conjecture. Irshad Manji makes the humorous point that the Koran's vision of seventy-two virgins being available in heaven for the martyr may rest on a mistake in translation. The word "virgins" should in fact be translated "white raisins"— so great a delicacy in seventh-century Arabia as to be considered heavenly fare! This would be similar to the Old Testament account of God's promise to Abraham of "a land flowing with milk and honey" (Exodus 3:8)—a literal interpretation of which would portray Israel as a paradise for dairy farmers and bee-keepers!

Whilst modern-day suicide bombers have been particularly linked to the Islamic faith, they are not, despite the pioneering efforts of Shii Hezbollah in Lebanon, confined to that religion. The tactic was also employed by Tamil suicide bombers of the 1990s in Sri Lanka, who before self-destruction pledged an oath to the Hindu god Shiva. In like manner, World War II Japanese kamikaze pilots invoked the Emperor-god on their suicide missions against enemy ships. The horror that occurred in New York on 11 September 2001 and in London on 7 July 2005 is, unfortunately, not a new phenomenon.[15] Convinced that they have a divine sanction to commit "a sacred attack," religious zealots will undertake any act of violence against any target to achieve their ends. Could it be only a matter of time before a Christian fundamentalist takes literally the injunctions in Deuteronomy 13:12–16 to destroy the heretic and his property by targeting what he perceives to be the infidel and his holy sites?

Be that as it may, Lloyd Geering is correct in observing that American Christian fundamentalists "do not need to resort to force, for the nation they belong to does it for them."[16] However, a reasonable fear remains that some of them will conclude that the government is not showing enough of God's wrath to those who worship other deities. When a conservative Christian televangelist Pat Robertson calls for the US government to assassinate a democratically elected foreign head-of-state, the Venezuelan President, Hugo Chavez, it is a warning sign that fundamentalists are getting out of control. And the "Crusader" mentality can operate at the micro- as well as the macro-level; the Oklahoma bombing of 1995 and Timothy McVeigh's alleged links to the white supremacist group "Elohim City" are evidence enough of that. If this atrocity that killed 168 and injured more than 500 people were repeated by right-wing Christian fundamentalists against Muslims, in America or elsewhere, the results could well be seen by hundreds of thousands to have ushered in the "End Time" that so many of them accept as an imminent reality. In fact, many actually believe that we are presently living in the End Time, and that very soon the Son of Man will return, the righteous will enter heaven, and sinners will be condemned to eternal hellfire. The four horsemen of the Apocalypse are saddling up, and we might as well urge them on, because the final conflict is about to begin. Like it or not, we need to recognize that we are in a race to put an end to such dangerous beliefs.

In his best-selling book, *The End of Faith*, Sam Harris has cogently argued that reason must replace faith. By its very nature religious faith inclines toward the demonic and, as he persuasively suggests, has resulted in such carnage and genocide that sane people are left with only one option—abandon religion altogether. Moreover, he pours scorn not only on the religious fundamentalist, but also on those who advocate "religious moderation." He condemns liberal theologians for their lack of critical thinking and their use of religion as a crutch to overcome the fear of death, the promotion of happiness or to give life meaning. The use of "God" as a consoling principle or as a mysterious force that no one can fathom ("God works in a mysterious way, his wonders to perform") is absurd and irrational. When liberal theologians have nothing to say about the purposes of a God to those seventy or more thousands who died as a result of a natural disaster like the earthquake which struck in the Kashmir province between Pakistan and India on October 8, 2005, then liberal theology is shown to be vacuous and empty. Both the liberal and fundamentalist are guilty of hiding behind faith in the light of overwhelming evidence that God does not exist. Faith is nothing more than the license religious people give themselves to keep believing when the opposite is the case. Moreover, for the fundamentalist, faith is often a license to kill. To solve the impasse and to avoid the destruction of the world, he insists, we must dispense with religious dogma and require our beliefs to conform to reason:

> This world is simply ablaze with bad ideas. There are still places where people are put to death for imaginary crimes—like blasphemy—and where the totality of a child's education consists of his learning to recite from an ancient book of religious fiction. There are countries where women are denied almost every human liberty, except the liberty to breed. And yet, these same societies are quickly acquiring terrifying arsenals of advanced weaponry. If we cannot inspire the developing world, and the Muslim world in particular, to pursue ends that are compatible with a global civilization, then a dark future awaits all of us.[17]

For Harris reason is the opposite of faith. Spirituality is understood as a biological brain-based need that acknowledges a necessary commitment to this world and how we function appropriately in the company of others. Harris argues that Eastern mystical traditions have recognized this, whilst Western religions have swallowed the Platonic dualism of mind/body and spirit/matter. There is no real world or real self beyond this existence and everyone is "bound to one another" because of their common humanity. Harris has set a real challenge for those of us who choose to remain within religious traditions.

It is my contention in this book that reason and reasonable people *do* exist within religious traditions, especially within Christianity. Indeed, it will be my central concern to show that "without the voice of reason every religion is its own curse."[18] Moreover, I will demonstrate that there are many Christian theologians who have been attempting to make faith more reasonable. They have provoked the ire of many within the Churches and have often suffered contempt, isolation, and rejection. This book will focus specifically on those within the Christian tradition whose aim is not to end faith but to *reform* it so that both Christianity and the world as a whole will be better and more humane places. For contrary to popular opinion and despite the recent shift toward the religious right, many prophetic voices within both Christianity and Islam have called upon their religious traditions not only to recognize but to do something about their faulty vision and their misdeeds—and have done so without being pressured to remain silent.

The most substantive and courageous attacks on fundamentalism within the Islamic faith tradition have come from women, most notably Irshad Manji, Taslima Nasrin and Wafa Sultan. In *The Trouble with Islam Today*, Irshad Manji writes what she describes as an "open letter" to her fellow Muslims to propose the revival of the Islamic concept of "ijtihad"—the tradition of independent thinking and questioning. Indeed, only minor shifts in thinking would be required for the present-day fundamentalist manifestation of Islam to be replaced by a reasonable faith that could engage in dialogue with other religious traditions. The Syrian born Wafa Sultan goes a step further. In a forthcoming book she goes so far as to question teachings of the Koran in an attempt to liberate Muslims from being held hostage to outdated ways of thinking.[19] And in a provocative interview with the Arabic news network, Al Jazeera, she questions Huntingdon's assertion of a clash of civilizations:

> The clash we are witnessing around the world is not a clash of religions or a clash of civilizations. It is a clash between two opposites, between two eras. It is a clash between a mentality that belongs to the Middle Ages and another mentality that belongs to the twenty-first century. It is a clash between civilization and backwardness, between the civilized and the primitive, between barbarity and rationality. It is a clash between freedom and oppression, between democracy and dictatorship. It is a clash between human rights, on the one hand and violation of these rights on the other. It is a clash between those who treat women like beasts and those who treat them like human beings. What we see today is not a clash of civilizations. Civilizations do not clash, but compete.[20]

Wafa Sultan's criticism of Islam derives from its refusal to update its thinking, its division of Muslim from non-Muslim, its support of suicide bombers and terrorism (her medical professor was shot in front of her eyes by the Muslim Brotherhood) and its subjection of women. Finding all of this fundamentally barbaric, she has renounced Islam, declaring herself to be "a secular human being." Her plea is for Muslims to critique their holy book and faith teachings. She has urged female Muslims to enter the front door of mosques and pray in the same room as the men. Likewise, the Bangladeshi writer Taslima Nasrin has rejected the faith of her birth. In both her autobiography *Meyebela* and the novel *Shame*, Nasrin reveals the terror that religion plays in the lives of its adherents and advocates humanism as the new religion. Her words reprise those of Wafa Sultan:

> Humankind is facing an uncertain future. The probability of new kinds of rivalry and conflict looms large. In particular, the conflict is between two different ideas, secularism and fundamentalism. I don't agree with those who

think the conflict is between two religions, namely Christianity and Islam, or Judaism and Islam. After all there are fundamentalists in every religious community. I don't agree with those people who think that the crusades of the Middle Ages are going to be repeated soon. Nor do I think that this is a conflict between the East and the West. To me, this conflict is basically between modern, rational, logical thinking and irrational, blind faith. To me, this is a conflict between modernity and anti-modernism. While some strive to go forward, others strive to go backward. It is a conflict between the future and the past, between innovation and tradition, between those who value freedom and those who do not.[21]

All three women have been condemned by Islamic fundamentalists and face death threats; two have been hounded out their homelands. They represent those who refuse to be crushed by an oppressive religious regime. Despite having been born into a faith system that treats their gender as inferior, they have seized hold of the Enlightenment project that values the emancipation of women, freedom from fear of heresy, and sexual expression. They write to encourage others of their faith to free themselves from the shackles of subjugation and to protest persecution and injustice. Despite the danger to their own lives they will not be silenced and enjoin others to combat religious fundamentalism. What is currently unfolding in Islam, then, is a struggle over what kind of Islam will triumph—conservative or liberal. In many ways what I attempt in this book is to create a Christian echo to these brave, prophetic Muslim voices.

Whilst all the evidence within the Western world points towards the decline in church attendance, the end of faith is not, as Harris suggests, imminent. Faith has proved to be more resilient than the doomsday prophets of its demise have recognized. Moreover, the status of faith across the spectrum of all religious traditions is not as homogeneous as Harris would have it. Likewise, he is wrong in arguing that the conservatives are the only voices that can be heard within religious traditions. I will argue that despite their disquieting effect, many liberal religious voices are being and deserve to be heard; indeed, their names should be trumpeted in the very cause that Harris so strenuously promotes—reasonable faith.[22] Furthermore the reformation of the world's religions from *within* each religion is the *only* way that religions will cease becoming centers of mistrust and hate. Indeed, the religion that never hears the cry of 'Heresy!' from within its own walls is dead. As Irshaj Manji admits:

> For too long, we Muslims have been sticking fingers in our ears and chanting 'Islam means peace' to drown out the negative noise from our holy book. Far better to own up to it. Not erase or revise, just recognize it and thereby join moderate Jews and Christians in confessing 'sins of Scripture,' as an American

bishop says about the Bible. In doing so, Muslims would show a thoughtful side that builds trust with the wider communities of the West.[23]

It is my aim in this book to confront the terrifying and destructive side on my own religion and to show that a peaceful alternative exists.

Malise Ruthven has correctly claimed that the rise of fundamentalism is a response to the threats implied by globalization, or more specifically, "to the anxieties generated by the thought that there are ways of living and believing other than those deemed to have been decreed by one's own group version of the deity."[24] The only effective place to begin the process of releasing those anxieties is to start the process of theological deconstruction within each religion. The claims of religions and their holy texts must be held up to scrutiny and reasoned debate. Only when religions recognize that they are human creations, having parochial origins and rooted in specific historical and cultural settings, can progress towards dialogue and respect can take place. Religious people must encounter what Don Cupitt has labeled: "religion-shock." This occurs when

> someone who is a strong and sincere believer in her own faith confronts, without evasion and without being able to explain it away, the reality of an entirely different form of faith, and faces the consequent challenge to her own deepest assumptions.[25]

This is what it means to live in global postmodernity—a world in which religious difference cannot be ignored, and therefore must be confronted with respect and dialogue. Exclusivist claims by the world's religions must be scrutinized and debated. Religious tribalism has no place in the new global market-place. Perhaps the gravest danger facing the world is that people might retreat into religious fundamentalism, adopt a fortress mentality, and seek security in ideological ramparts. Too much is at stake for us to sit idly by and let this happen.[26]

Sam Harris' apprehensiveness at the threat of religious terrorism mirrors the concerns of three of the most outspoken contemporary Christian theologians—Don Cupitt, Lloyd Geering and John Shelby Spong. These writers have confronted the traditional claims of their faith in the light of recent epistemological, scientific, and literary-critical methodologies. Simply put: how can Christianity make sense to educated rational people?

Significantly, they have acknowledged that the old theistic God has died. They ponder what kind of Christianity will emerge when its supernatural underpinning is questioned or doubted. Like Harris, they have squarely faced the science versus religion question and wondered how it is possible to speak of "God" today. In the aftermath of the tsunami(s) that recently devastated much of Southeast Asia and Africa and left 300,000 people dead, is it reasonable to conceive of God as the creative power behind the world and its natural forces? Would it not be more seemly to wonder whether such a God makes any sense at all? As the biologist and Darwinian Richard Dawkins eloquently expresses it,

> Not only does science know why the tsunami happened, it can give precious hours of warning. If a small fraction of the tax breaks handed out to churches, mosques and synagogues had been diverted into an early warning system, tens of thousands of people, now dead, would have been moved to safety. Let's get up off our knees, stop cringing before bogeymen and virtual fathers, face reality, and help science to do something constructive about human suffering.[27]

What, then, are the options for Christianity when God becomes a problem? Christian theologians have developed two quite different concepts to resolve the crisis in belief about God. The first is called panentheism, and is illustrated most tellingly in the books of Bishop John Shelby Spong. It might be described as the essence of "liberal Christianity." The second approach, more controversial, is surprisingly close to that proposed by Harris. Often labeled "non-realism," it is central to the writings of Don Cupitt and Lloyd Geering. It characterizes "radical Christianity." In later chapters I will analyze these theories and their roots and recount the theological odysseys that these thinkers have undertaken in the process of synthesizing the work of the most important philosophers and theologians of the last two centuries. Moreover, I will seek to demonstrate an important link between Geering and Cupitt's religious naturalism and the work of such leading biologists as Ursula Goodenough. Indeed, Harris' appeal for an ethics that takes into account our biological knowledge is answered by what Goodenough labels her "credo of continuation," namely that "concepts central to religious thought are in fact operant throughout the biological world."[28] Goodenough's religious naturalism can offer a meaningful vision of a post-theistic ethical way of life.

However, as Harris himself suggests, "faith" is more than belonging to a particular religion. The faith of people in the third millennium is a much more complex phenomenon than it is commonly portrayed to be. Although the usual assumption is that the battle-lines—especially in America—are drawn between liberalism and fundamentalism, this divide is only part of a wide panorama of religious choice that has been aptly termed "the Divine Supermarket."[29] Indicative of this new religious state of affairs is the fact that in the western world, the word religion is slowly becoming replaced by the word "spiritual."

I live in a country that has been described as the most secular and godless nation on earth. My Antipodean neighbors in New Zealand will dispute that claim, regarding that epithet as rightfully their own, but the notable antipathy towards religious identity in both countries masks a spiritual search that follows many diverse paths. Judging from the resilience of indigenous religious systems emphasizing ancestral spirits and the popularity of a plethora of 'New Age' paths, as well as Wicca, pagan, and earth-based religions that are presently the fastest growing spiritualities, Australians and New Zealanders have not abandoned the search for spiritual meaning. Rather, their adoption of a huge variety of spiritual options is part of a widespread rejection of organized religions and the rise of what has been labeled "grassroots spirituality"—which, if the research is correct, promises to demonstrate in the not-too-distant future far greater numbers of adherents than the world's "standard" religions. In fact, many argue that "a spirituality revolution" is taking place in the western world. It is being fueled by those at the "grassroots," that is, by those ordinary folk who are moving away from the historic religions and forging their own spiritual paths using both new and ancient traditions. What I will call a "smorgasbord of therapeutic spiritualities" is available for people to pick and choose from, and for many there is no need to cross the threshold of the Church. I will also show that the media's polarization of religion into fundamentalism and secularism is misleading. We inhabit a much more diverse religious landscape than is generally portrayed. It may be true that in the West the major religions are in decline, but it is also evident that the newer spiritualities are becoming increasingly popular.

In short, this book seeks to address what I see as the central issue in a world that may seem headed for a catastrophe brought about by dissonance amongst the present world religions. If you want it in a nutshell, it is the problem of God. I write as a committed member of my own faith community—Christianity—who is concerned that its recent take-over by extremists can inspire some of its leaders to say the most appalling things from their pulpits:

> We must stop the stupidity of stretching social tolerance into religious or philosophical relativism . . . different religions cannot all be right. **Some, or all of them, are wrong. And if wrong are monstrous lies and deceits of Satan—devised to destroy the life of the believers.**[30]

Such sentiments have no place in a postmodern world where religious tolerance should be a hallmark of *all* religious traditions. But to create such an atmosphere, one that leads to racial and cultural harmony, *depends on each religion's repudiating its own self-imposed limits* that divide the world into 'us' and 'them'. It is my aim to show that in the case of Christianity this can be done quite easily and that some theologians have been actively pursuing just such an end for many years. But in addition the dark side of religion must be expunged in order to permit the flowering of a new era of religious harmony. My most cherished hope is that it is not too late to attempt this reformation.

So what would Christianity look like if we begin to tinker with ideas of God? What kind of Christianity emerges? The questions that I will specifically address are these:

- How can we believe in or even talk about God in a meaningful way in a pluralist world?
- Is the Christian story locked into belief in a supernatural someone or something, or can it be reformed or restructured by new understandings of who/what God is?
- What will the Christianity of the future look like?

Let's begin with Bishop Spong and panentheism, and the options that he offers for a future faith . . .

# 2

## PANENTHEISM
## JOHN SHELBY SPONG

The retired Episcopalian Bishop of Newark, the Right Reverend John Shelby Spong, is a liberal Christian evangelist *par excellence*. In books such as *Rescuing the Bible from Fundamentalism, Living in Sin, Why Christianity Must Change or Die, A New Christianity for a New World,* and the very latest *The Sins of Scripture,* he has contested religious conservatives both in the United States and throughout the world. His autobiography, *Here I Stand,* records a lifelong struggle to correct ecclesiastical and social inequality. He has resolutely campaigned for radically inclusive churches and societies: those that are opposed to racism, sexism, and dogmatism. He has consistently identified himself with the "Church alumni association" or the "believers-in-exile":

> I am one of a countless host of modern men and women for whom traditional religious understandings have lost most of their ancient power. We are that silent majority of believers who find it increasingly difficult to remain members of the Church and still be thinking people.[1]

This concern for those who have been alienated from the Christian Church by fundamentalist teaching has shaped his ministry and writing. One of the reasons why many people are reluctant to step inside a church, he contends, is that they are too often required to "have brain surgery to be faithful Christians."[2] Countless churches have a serious problem with religious literacy because many members of the clergy and laity alike fail to face the challenges posed by scientific and Enlightenment thinking. But all is not lost: it is still possible to create a more reasonable faith, a new Christianity that will not go the way of the dinosaur.

In this chapter I will highlight five issues that underlie Spong's concerns, in each case pointing out his principal resources for change and his vision of the future of Christianity.

For reasonably well-educated people, the first stumbling block to Christian belief is that churches have promoted redundant ways of understanding or interpreting the nature of God. This has resulted in what he calls "the end of theism."

### GOD: END OF THEISM

For Spong, the God-problem centers on a definition of "God" that it is too narrow, too tribal and too sectarian. This is a major cause in the decline of

23

the churches because people find more engaging and inclusive ideas of the divine elsewhere, especially in what is often referred to as "New Age spirituality."[3] He states that eighty percent of the population in Western societies has no link to the Church whilst a mere twenty percent are members. This is, of course, nearly the reverse of the situation described in Luke's parable of the farmer who has ninety-nine sheep safely in the sheep-fold and goes to search for the one that is lost. In the postmodern world Western Christianity must face the distasteful fact that the Church has little impact upon the lives of an increasingly secularized populace.

The first four chapters of Spong's *A New Christianity for a New World* aim at redefining the Christian understanding of God. It is important to note that his vision of a new Christianity flows from this redefinition of God necessitated by what he epigrammatically terms "the end of theism."[4] What this latter term means can be seen clearly in the first of his twelve modern-day theses.

In 2000, in a plea for a new reformation of the Christian faith, Spong followed the example of the sixteenth century reformer, Martin Luther, by composing a list of theses that would outline the faith of the future. Unlike Luther, who nailed ninety-five theses to the doors of a German Cathedral in 1517, Spong used the latest computer technology to post his twelve propositions on the Internet. The unabridged version of the first one can be found in *Here I Stand*:

> Theism, as a way of defining God, is dead. God can no longer be understood with credibility as a Being, supernatural in power, dwelling above the sky and prepared to invade human history periodically to enforce the divine will. So, most theological God-talk today is meaningless unless we find a new way to speak of God.[5]

Some of his critics have seized on this to say that he now is espousing atheism and doesn't believe in an objective God, but Spong responds by affirming that God is very real to him. He is not denying the existence of God, but discarding the traditional theistic understanding of God as a supernatural being that dwells somewhere "out there." He makes a distinction between the culturally formulated explanations about God and the God that people experience. All explanations of God are human constructs, but the fact that there is so much God-talk indicates that there is a greater reality to which the word God points. He calls himself a "God-intoxicated" person and insists that the experience of an objective God is real.

So, what does Spong mean by "the God experience"? This is to enter the very heart of Spong's life-long religious search. Repeatedly in his books he insists that God is real and that this God is "not a person, but the source of that power that nurtures personhood, not a being, but the Ground of Being, the source from which all being flows."[6] For him the "God-experience" is ultimately holy and real.

How did Spong arrive at this idea of God? What are his sources? In order to understand his theological odyssey one has to return to the turbulence of the 1960s. Indeed, his theological perspective might be labeled "a theology of the '60s." In particular, he was influenced by someone who, like himself, was a liberal Anglican/Episcopalian Bishop, and who attracted controversy through his writings—the Right Reverend John A. T. Robinson. The book that brought Bishop Robinson media recognition was a small paperback entitled *Honest to God*. Written in 1963, it was only 143 pages in length, but in his preface to *A New Christianity*, Spong declares that "*Honest to God* shaped my theological journey decisively" and that the purpose of writing *A New Christianity* was to "move forward the work begun in the last century by a man who was my mentor and my friend."[7] In order to understand Spong, then, we need to be conversant with John Robinson and his sources of inspiration.

Robinson was influenced by two philosopher-theologians: one was Paul Tillich, a German/American, and the other Dietrich Bonhoeffer, a German who was executed by the Nazis just prior to the conclusion of World War II.

The title of chapter 2 of *Honest to God* is "The End of Theism," a phrase by which Robinson intends that the classical, supernatural understanding of God has now come to an end. He announces that Christians have "come of age" and it is time to discard the traditional thinking about God. The medieval understanding of God was of the God of the three-decker Universe (the waters under the earth, earth, and the heavens above), a concept that promoted belief in a deity beyond the known world—a distant supernatural God. This warped cosmology had led to the mechanical universe of eighteenth and nineteenth century deism, whose most famous exponent, William Paley, proposed that God had crafted the world like a large watch and, after winding it up, he had allowed it to it run its course, discreetly maintaining his distance and being uninvolved in its day-to-day operation. For Robinson, this remote, supernatural God was not one in whom Christians of the twentieth century could readily believe. This faith had to be replaced with a more apposite understanding of God, one that was in tune with modern ideas of science. To this end he appropriated the writings of Paul Tillich and Dietrich Bonhoeffer.

Robinson embraced two ideas about God from Tillich's influential work, *The Courage to Be*. First, he adopted Tillich's notion that "God" was not limited solely to the Christian revelation. There was, as Tillich phrased it, "the God above the God of theism"—a God who transcends *all* religions. It is noteworthy that this pluralist paradigm of a divine Being who is greater than all religious manifestations has now gained widespread acceptance in theological circles. It was popularized by the theologian/philosopher John Hick in his seminal book, *God and the Universe of Faiths*, where he argued that a theological Copernican revolution must occur. God and not the human messenger—Jesus, Mohammed or Siddhartha Gautama—must be the true centre of religious devotion. All religions revolve around God, and the experience of God is foundational to belief. Religions reflect varying human responses to the one divine reality. As the Quaker-Anglican hymn writer, Sydney Carter, expresses it:

> Every star shall sing a carol
> Every creature high or low
> Come and praise the king of heaven
> **By whatever name you know. . . .**

Second, in order to counter the idea of a remote God, Robinson borrowed a concept from Tillich and argued that God should be called "the Ground of Our Being." God is not met "out there," or "at the borders of life," but is reached "at its centre." In this he also appropriated Dietrich Bonhoeffer's idea of "religionless Christianity." By using this phrase, Bonhoeffer did not mean the end of Christianity, but rather sought to contrast the true nature of Christianity with "false religion," which he defined as a restrictive understanding that limited religion to the individual, the spiritual realm, or the field of speculative metaphysics. Bonhoeffer's true religion involved the discovery that

- God is "the beyond in the midst of life". We locate God in the everyday experience of life. We find God in what we know, not what we don't know.
- God is not just the Almighty Lord, uninvolved in the lives of people, but also a God who can be powerless and weak, and who in the Jesus story allows himself to be crucified to bring about a better world.
- True discipleship is the art of holy worldliness. It is not to be found in cultivating asceticism, but by serving God by way of creating a more just and humane world.
- The church is not a religious sanctuary or a sheltered enclave; rather it is "to stand in the centre of the city" where it must witness to a transformation of society.

By conflating the thoughts of Tillich and Bonhoeffer, we can see that Robinson was promoting what is termed "Panentheism"—the proposition that God is found in everything in the world, but cannot be defined only in terms of the world. God is the Ground of Being who is beyond all our images. We must not look outwards or upwards to find God, but rather focus our attention at the very centre of life. From this it follows that God is not separate from humanity. Robinson argued that the existence of God could not be proved, but his character could be recognized in people's actions. And therefore, because of our holy worldliness, we are responsible for doing the God-work of establishing the kingdom or the realm of God. This idea gave rise in the 1960s and '70s to many Christians who fused the Christian Gospel with Marxist ideology to promote what became known as "the social gospel." As a result of this new imperative to social and political justice, many Anglican and Roman Catholic priests in Europe became "worker-priests." Some even left the priesthood altogether to enroll in the new discipline of sociology, and thus gaining entry into a kind of social work that became known as "the secular priesthood."[8] This movement made popular the catch-phrase "orthopraxis" (right action), rather than "orthodoxy" (right belief), and priests became actively involved in demanding improved public and employment benefits for the underprivileged and marginalized of society. This is powerfully illustrated by John Robinson's widow, Ruth, in a retrospective assessment of her husband's theology:

> Just before New Year I was returning home across London after a Christmas visit. On an underground stairway a small thin boy was huddled in a corner. His face was grey and his eyes looked desperate and hopeless. A piece of cardboard was lying on the ground beside him. Among the pennies scattered on it two words were written: 'Change please.' The child was asking only for money. How could *he* see the world as [Thomas] Traherne once saw it, or hope for such a change in his? But nothing less than this is enough. **The Kingdom of God is a vision of our world transformed. To enter it we must unlearn the dirty devices of cynicism, apathy, greed. The love of God is a vision of the human heart transformed, by compassion, hope and trust. We change the world by loving it for the sake of every child.** Without a compassionate vision we are dead. We must trust it enough to follow where it leads.[9]

Spong's writing is filled with echoes of John Robinson and his sources. This is clearest in his endorsement of the "realm of God" theology, which proposes that God is realized in social action and in combating inequality on behalf of all those who are on the margins of church and society. Original sin is a myth, but evil is real, and is to be understood as that which prevents people from being whole or living life to the full—whether its root cause is hatred, poverty, oppression, lack of opportunity, or discrimination due to race, gender or sexuality. Bonhoeffer's holy worldliness is promoted by Spong as "loving wastefully, living fully," and to expand the presence of love is to advance the work of the kingdom:

> The messiah we need today is some random act of kindness, some bold proposal to close the hole in the ozone layer, some discreet move to include candor into politics, some new intensive care for the planet. Perhaps the messiah will come when we have broken bread with our enemies.[10]

The outcome of Spong's use of Robinson, Tillich and Bonhoeffer is the affirmation that God is real, but is beyond all our images, both mental and physical. We can experience God, but can't define God. God is a symbol for that which is immortal, invisible, and timeless. As Spong says:

> It was Tillich who . . . was to shape me theologically. God was not a person to Tillich. God was the Ground of Being, unknowable, mysterious, without form. Most people do not worship God, said Tillich. They worship, rather, a human creation endowed with supernatural qualities. He spoke of the God beyond the gods of men and women. He correlated God with being, Christ with existence and Holy Spirit with church. I struggled with concepts I had never heard before. My personal God, a kind of divine father protector, a bit of a Mr. Fixit, what Dietrich Bonhoeffer would later call the God of the gaps, began to shake visibly, to wobble before my eyes, and to fade perceptibly. I had begun my long theological journey into maturity.[11]

### JESUS

Once the concept of God has been enlarged, then the rest of the traditional Christian message must be amended to fit it. Spong paints a new portrait of Jesus, because if the classical idea of God is dead, so must the traditional concept of Jesus. He labels Jesus—"the boundary-breaker":

> What I see is a new portrait of Jesus. He is the one who was more deeply and fully alive than anyone else I have ever encountered, whether in my life-time, in history, or in literature. I see him pointing towards something he calls the realm (or kingdom) of God, where new possibilities demand to be considered. I see him portrayed as one who was constantly dismantling the barriers that separate people from one another. I see him inviting his followers to join with him, to walk without fear beyond those security boundaries that always prohibit, block, or deny our access to a deeper humanity. Perhaps above all else he is for me a boundary-breaker who enables me to envision the possibility of my own humanity breaking through my human barriers to reach the divinity that his life reveals.[12]

To a world like the one I have outlined in chapter 1, polarized by social, economic, and religious discord, Spong offers a Jesus who breaks down the barriers of religious and social tribalism. Jesus envisaged the establishment of a new society that would erase the antiquated boundaries that segregate people: class, ethnicity, gender, and religion. Jesus was the initiator of a radical, transformative movement that was boundary-breaking and totally inclusive. In a post-September 11 world, here is good news waiting to be heard: the religious and social divisions that currently bedevil the world can be swiftly eradicated. In the person of Jesus, Christians can find a "God-presence" who "relativizes every barrier that blocks our wholeness and makes us God-bearers too." The radical demand of Jesus is that "all people seek the path of wholeness into a new humanity." Jesus, then, is a doorway into the God who is beyond all attempts to define God.

It is at this point that conservative Christians step forward and demand to know whether Jesus is "the only way to God." Because of his definition of God, Spong's answer is an unequivocal negative: the 'God above the God of theism' proclaimed by Tillich cannot be restricted to the Christian revelation. Moreover, the presence of God is often transmitted by people outside the boundaries historically set by the Christian Church—such powerful spiritual presences as the Buddha, Mahatma Ghandi, Thich Nhat Hanh and Dag Hammarskjöld. Thus Christian claims for the divinity of Jesus fade as the savior becomes a doorway for Christians to open in search of God, but many other entrances remain available for non-Christians. It should be noted that Spong does not advocate the abolition of religious identity or the amalgamation of all religious traditions into something akin to the Baha'i religion. Rather each religious faith should acknowledge the others as valid ways into the presence of the holy God who is beyond and greater than all religious expressions.

Of course, this way of understanding Jesus has other important implications for Christianity. Other theological dominos must come clattering down, and in particular the injunction at the end of St. Luke's Gospel that Christians must proselytize every nation in the name of the Trinitarian God.

### BEYOND EVANGELISM TO POST-THEISTIC UNIVERSALISM

Christianity and Islam have been the two religions most committed to the expansion of their faith by the conversion of those they traditionally viewed as heathens. The Christian missionary endeavor has taken the Christian Gospel into most parts of the world, often with an urgency demanding an immediate decision: conversion or damnation. Spong calls for this practice to cease. He enjoins an end to "decades of evangelism" and the intentional conversion of those of other faiths. Christianity is not the sole pathway to God. Whilst he is content that his own adoption of Western Christianity has led him to experience God, he views this as an historical accident. He was born in the West and his understanding of God has been both nurtured by and filtered through a particular religious tradition (Anglicanism). He concedes that we should not be constrained by our traditions, but rather use them as inherited receptacles within which to explore the reality of the God who is beyond all religious traditions. Moreover, he hopes that each member of the other religious traditions will take a similarly pluralist approach to worship the God beyond God. He cites with approval Matthew Fox's metaphor for God as groundwater. No matter how diverse the locations from which it is drawn, it still has the same source. The necessity for evangelism is replaced by "post-theistic universalism" whereby the tribalism of the past fades into oblivion. Instead of different religions vying for supremacy, they will be united in exploring more deeply their experience of God as love:

> My hope is that my brothers and sisters who find Judaism, Islam, Hinduism or Buddhism as their point of entry, based upon their time and place in history, will also explore their pathway into God in a similar manner, until they too can escape the limits of their tradition at its depths and, grasping the essence of their system's religious insights, move on to share that essence with me and all the world. Then each of us, clinging to the truth, the pearl of great price if you will, that we have found in the spiritual wells from which we have drunk, can reach across the once insuperable barriers to share as both givers and receivers in the riches present in all human sacred traditions.[13]

The obvious question that arises from this pluralist paradigm is whether other religions have the capacity to act likewise. To what degree do other religions have the capacity to become liberal? Is Christianity the only faith tradition that has the capability to reinvent itself? How would other religious traditions react to the suggestion that their revelation of God is not unique?

## PRAYER

Having abandoned the theistic God who intervenes directly in the lives of people, has Spong then dispensed with prayer? First off, he dismisses the notion of prayer as a sort of shopping list given to God asking for A, B and C in return for our having been virtuous. But he does accept prayer as meditation or contemplation. That does not mean, of course, that prayer is simply an exercise in self-knowledge or arriving at passive acceptance of the status quo. For Spong self-knowledge gained though meditation is linked to active service of others. The biblical profession that God is love (1John 3) can be reversed: love is God. Thus the God who is the ground of being is revealed by the love shown by human beings towards others. God is made visible not by a supernatural revelation, but by the human acts of loving wastefully and living fully. As he says in a section written whilst staying at the home of the late John Robinson,

> Prayer is what I am doing when I live wastefully, passionately and wondrously and invite others to do so with me or even because of me. Prayer is also the struggle for human justice. It is the fight to remove killing stereotypes, to hurl back the ignorance of prejudice, and to protect the holiness of God's creation.[14]

Thus prayer is linked to active involvement in social, economic and political processes. In his spiritual response to the destruction of September 11, Spong argues that in such a context true prayer would be to refrain from invoking God's punishment. We must reject the old supernatural image of the vengeful God of hatred who escalates the cycle of violence. Instead, we must act out our prayer by being the God-presence committed to a more loving and just world.[15] Thus, he can "pray constantly, but . . . pray nontheistically. My goal in life is to pray without ceasing, which means that I seek to be a God-presence in every relationship I enter."[16]

How then does this new way of being Christian affect institutional Christianity and what will the Church of the future to look like?

### THE *ECCLESIA* OF THE FUTURE

It is hardly surprising that Spong's program for the reformation of Christianity should have left him with ambivalent feelings about the Christian Church that he served in the high office of Diocesan Bishop of Newark (1976–2000). Prior to publication of *A New Christianity for a New World* Spong had flippantly commented to television viewers that he was a clergyman who didn't find church-folk too much to his liking or that his principal audience was the church-alumni association.[17] Despite these comments, however, he had remained wedded to the church as an institution that was a force for good and at least potentially an agency of radicalism. But since his retirement from ecclesiastical office, his condemnation of institutional Christianity has become more pronounced:

> I am now convinced that institutional Christianity has become so consumed by its quest for power and authority, most of which is rooted in the exclusive claims for the Bible, that the authentic voice of God can no longer be heard within it. So I want to invite people to a mountaintop where together we can watch the mighty wind, the earthquake and the fire destroy those idols of creed, scripture and church, all of which have been used to hide us from the reality of God. When that destruction is complete, my hope is that we too will then be ready to hear that still, small voice of calm that bids us to return to that vocation which is, I believe, the essence of what it means to be a disciple of Jesus.[18]

Spong's challenge is that we should move into exile from the institutional church for the sake of a reformed and reinvigorated faith community. The church is no longer sustainable, he says, and he urges us to set out on the journey into a new community that he labels the future ecclesia. Ecclesia is a neutral term for those who have been "called out" as opposed to those who "go to" the church, synagogue, and mosque. His call for the formation of such a body is based on two premises. The first is that people need to gather together as a community of those "who have been called out limits, out of prejudices, out of brokenness, out of self-centeredness." The second is that these people will thereby be called into life, love, being, wholeness and God.

Spong argues that the future need for religious communities will be assured by the natural desire that people have for connectedness with each other and with the sacred Presence that lives at the centre of everything:

> Father God and Mother Church will be no more. But human beings will always worship, seek the Holy together in community, and gather as a family might to remember who they are, to recall their origins, and to seek help in becoming all that they can be. It will be in the doing of these things that the church of the future will be born.[19]

The hallmarks of the future ecclesia will be:

- Jesus (*and others*) as an exemplar of divinized humanity
- Renunciation of guilt as an instrument of control
- An open-ended quest for unfolding truth
- Mutual care and support in times of crisis
- Rituals to honor the special moments in life, and
- Leadership that has escaped the clericalism of the past.[20]

### CONCLUSION

It can be seen that for Spong the "God-presence" is very real and that it forms the basis of his faith for the future. Each religious tradition is a response to the God-experience and a modality for establishing communities of care and love for those who seek after truth. The God who is revealed through the religious traditions is greater than the individual traditions themselves. All faith stories will be celebrated and all sacred scriptures accepted, not as ultimate revelation, but as complementary guides to finding God. This is the God beyond God, the Ground of Being. Jesus is the doorway into the Ground of Being for those who inhabit the Christian tradition. Other religious traditions will have different doorways. For Spong, Jesus' message was one of radical inclusivity; he revealed a God who breaks every barrier and prejudice. One day, the religious barriers will be swept away to be replaced by a God-filled humanity, which is "wonderfully diverse, yearning to live, eager to love, daring and wanting to journey in community into the wonder and mystery of the God who is Being itself."[21]

Perhaps Spong's mantra sums up his reformation of Christianity:

**God is the Source of Life who is worshipped when we live fully,**

**God is the Source of Love who is worshipped when we love wastefully,**

**God is the Ground of Being who is worshipped when we have the courage to be.**

# 3

## NON-REALISM
## DON CUPITT AND LLOYD GEERING

This third chapter will examine how Don Cupitt and Lloyd Geering have responded to the "God problem." Whilst they differ in approach and emphasis—Geering paints on a global and historical canvas, whereas Cupitt's style is more impressionistic and existential—they are in full agreement that the problem posed by "the end of theism" calls for a much more radical interpretation than that outlined by John Shelby Spong (see chapter 2). Their revolutionary stance has been labelled "theological non-realism." As is the case with Spong and his redefinition of God, the non-realism of Geering and Cupitt also produces a domino effect by raising additional issues about the future of Christianity and the Church.

Don Cupitt relates in the first episode ('The Mechanical Universe') of his BBC TV series, "Sea of Faith," how he encountered the "God problem." The trigger for Cupitt's redefinition of God was a pastoral encounter. As a young assistant minister fresh out of the academic "ivory tower" of Cambridge University, he was assigned in the early 1960s to serve as curate to the less than affluent parishioners of St. Philip's Anglican Church, Salford. One of his tasks was to act as a Chaplain to the local hospital, and in the course of visiting patients he found himself beset by religious difficulties when obliged to endorse supernatural explanations of people's medical problems. How could he possibly repeat the prescribed prayers from the Anglican Book of Common Prayer to those who were sick? How could he tell a man dying of cancer that this devastating sickness had been sent by God? Could he bite his tongue and agree that the birth of a handicapped child was a sign of God's displeasure, or should he insist on a secular medical interpretation? On most occasions, Cupitt reports, he summoned up the courage to offer the "natural causes" explanation—that their medical condition was best described and managed by Western medicine, rather than by any supernatural causation or divine intervention. Indeed, religion was not some kind of "auxiliary technology" to be wheeled in when medicine and the surgeons had failed. God was not a "god of the gaps" fortuitously available to fill in the cracks left by scientific knowledge. As a result of these encounters Cupitt was forced to redefine the task of religion in humanistic terms. At the very end of that first programme he states:

Religion was a way of affirming the value of human life, from the first breath to
the very last. It is up to us to give it that value: to affirm human dignity in the
face of the indifferent universe.[1]

To reformulate this as what I take to be Don Cupitt's "original vision," he saw
the need to free Christianity by replacing its supernatural underpinning with
what he calls a non-realist understanding of the Christian faith.

But what is non-realism? By non-realism I am referring to theological/
metaphysical non-realism. This is not the same as anti-realism, its philosophical counterpart with which it is often confused, and which holds that
the truths we use to interpret the universe are of our own making; that Truth
does not exist "out-there." Simply stated, theological non-realists interpret
religious language as an attempt to express our moral insights or our way of
viewing the world. The word "God" does not refer to an objective person or
thing, but is a verbal symbol we use to denote our highest moral or spiritual
values. "God" is not a Being over and above us, but is a conceptual creation
of the human mind.

The classic statement of this idea appeared in 1841 in the German theologian Ludwig Feuerbach's *The Essence of Christianity*. Feuerbach asserted
that the notion of a loving God was the human ideal of love projected onto
the Universe: "God" is love deified. Cupitt takes up Feuerbach's idea in
asserting that people must give up the realist idea of an all-powerful God
"out-there" who created and continues to sustain the universe. God is better
viewed as the personification of religious values. Non-realism stands midway
between realism and atheism. Unlike atheists who wish to abandon all God-
talk because it is self-delusory and realists who assert that the word refers
to someone/something greater than human beings, Cupitt seeks to affirm
religious language as expressive of our deepest concerns and highest ideals.
These ideals have intrinsic value. Religious language does not need to refer
to a divine being in order to have authority in our lives. Religious language
is a human creation that has value in itself without the need for any external
referent. The experience of God is, in large part, a function of own psycho-
logical projections. In short, we made up all the God-talk, but it is nonetheless very important talk.

Thus the word "God" need not be abandoned, for it represents a valu-
able fiction—or, if one prefers, a personification—that can be put to profit-
able use. Cupitt proposes that when people use the word "God" they refer
to a spiritual ideal: the word does not name a metaphysical Being, but the
concept can help people live *religiously*. Such a way of living would blend
the ethics of Christianity with the spirituality of Buddhism to create what
Richard Holloway has called a "godless morality." Christian doctrines are
not to be understood literally, but interpreted in terms of the way of life that

they recommend. To believe in God as Creator, for example, is to understand one's existence as pure and gracious gift; and to live a risen life is to proclaim: "Christ is risen—in me!" Indeed, all fundamental Christian doctrines can be interpreted in a non-realist way (see figure 1).

**Figure 1**
The Non-Realist interpretation of Christian doctrine

| Christian doctrine | Realist Interpretation (Traditional; dogmatic) | Non-realist interpretation |
|---|---|---|
| Creation | God as first cause of the world; God causes the "big bang." . . . | Life should be treated as pure gift. |
| Providence | God preordains and supervises the entire course of world-events, and of each life. | I believe that I will come through; my faith will not let me down. |
| Prayer | One seeks favor from a godfather. | Intercessory prayer as an expression of love and concern, and as a way of supporting the one prayed for. Prayer as attention to being. |
| Incarnation | The metaphysical son of god takes a human life as his own, and becomes its subject. | Jesus is seen as embodying the religious ideal; he is love in human form. |
| Resurrection | Jesus rises bodily from the tomb. | The believer who identifies himself with Jesus and dies with him in baptism rises to a new life. |
| Ascension | Jesus goes bodily up to heaven in the sky. | The believer elevates Jesus to the status of "lord" in his life. |
| Eternal life | Post-mortem life in heaven. | The "solar" living of the believer who is no longer afraid of death. |

Cupitt originally used this summary as a teaching aid with Undergraduates at the University of Cambridge. Naturally enough, students often desired to blend elements of realism and non-realism, but Cupitt would respond that it was an either/or scenario; they must choose from only one column. For Cupitt, the students were like liberal Christians who want it both ways—they are critical of traditional Christian ideas, but don't really challenge them. Radical non-realism is much more robust and academically defensible.

The non-realist position finds particularly effective expression in Anthony Freeman's insightful paradox: "I do believe in God, and one of the things I believe about God is that he does not exist."[2] By this he means that you can retain the Christian language but you must strip away the objectivity of God and rid the Church of its supernatural teachings in order to allow the emergence of a Christianity that is grounded in this world and therefore more in tune with modern thinking. This reformed Christianity can provide a framework for spirituality and ethics for humans who have, to use the radical catchphrase, "come of age." Cupitt describes it as Christian Buddhism: "the content, the spirituality and the values, are Christian; the form is Buddhist."[3] He is interested in Buddhism because it is a non-metaphysical form of religion that from its inception repudiated the idea of an objective deity. By "Christian Buddhism" he means a less dogmatic and ideological approach to religion, with a much more open-ended understanding and use of symbols and language.

With God thus redefined, the Church's house of cards comes tumbling down, and just as in the case of Spong's reformulation, new concepts and doctrines will be needed if Christianity is to survive. Since I have elsewhere presented a detailed exposition of Cupitt's non-realist reformation of Christianity,[4] I will here offer only a brief account of his vision for the future Church and its proclamation of faith.

In 1989 David Edwards in *Tradition and Truth* described Cupitt as having undergone something similar to a "Victorian clergyman's 'loss of faith'" and called for his resignation from the Anglican Church.[5] Cupitt replied that far from losing his faith, he had regained it! Edwards had quite missed Cupitt's point, which is not to eradicate the Church but to reform it. And the best way to reforming that institution is from inside. Moreover, he is able to stay within the Church as a non-realist because "Anglican formularies nowhere say either that the Church is infallible or irreformable, or that priests have got to be metaphysical realists."[6] It is a bold assertion, and surprisingly one that the Anglican Church authorities have never challenged Cupitt on, though sad to say Torquil Paterson in South Africa and Anthony Freeman in the United Kingdom have been put to the sword for similar statements. Paterson was a theological lecturer in an Anglican seminary in South Africa. He was forced to resign his position for expressing his admiration for Cupitt and non-realism. He wrote:

> Like Don Cupitt today, I contend that the only authentically modern way of conceiving God is as an abstract way of referring to all that is good in human life and community. Theology should be, therefore, the science of decoding traditional belief in a transcendent God in terms of a secular humanism.[7]

In like manner Freeman's bishop dismissed him from his parish for espousing non-realism in his book, *God in Us*. Not only can it prove harmful to one's reputation to be a theological non-realist, it might result in the loss of one's livelihood.

Reconceptualizing the Church was thus a major component of Cupitt's original vision, and this interest was reinforced five years later in *Radicals and the Future of the Church*, a book that set forth his vision of the Church to come.

In *Radicals and the Future of the Church* one of Cupitt's aims is to examine how it is still possible for the Church to exist in postmodernity. He identifies a conflict that many members of the Church have experienced—the clash between individual beliefs and the doctrines of the Church as they are interpreted by ecclesiastical authorities. He asks what recourse is available to church members who come to the realization that the Church has become an enemy of "truth and freedom." Should they leave, or carry on silently in accordance with their inner promptings, or make their thoughts and feelings clear to everyone? At one moment he is pessimistic, noting that all one can do is stay and attempt to reform the Church without expecting to have much success. Later, he becomes hopeful, joining the American a/theologian Mark C. Taylor, who in his book *Altarity* espouses the notion of new religious thought that exults in *différance*. There emerges a vision of a Church that

> will rejoice in being highly pluralistic, a tapestry of diverse Christianities all adding up to an aesthetically beautiful, morally-variegated and ever-changing whole. Why shouldn't the faith mean something different to each Christian?[8]

In 1989 Cupitt's proposal for remaining in the Church and reforming it *from within* has two main components—ethics and human relationships. Ethically speaking, the Church is needed because "it is a theatre in which we solemnly enact our deepest feelings about the human condition."[9] Furthermore, the churches have in the past served as a useful corrective to the power of the State, which has too often been a cruel and oppressive institution. They have exercised their prophetic role in defending humanitarian priorities and individual human rights; their value system, rooted as it is in love, can serve to counterbalance the cold utilitarianism of the state. Thus, lacking a powerful objective God, Cupitt resorts to an argument from antiquity: the churches are ancient organizations that have stood the test of time as fraternities embodying communitarian values that can challenge and even frustrate oppressive power structures. The obvious retort to this is that the churches have exhibited just as much authoritarianism as the State, and have themselves often employed the very abuses with which they have charged the State. To take one example from my own country, the churches in Australia are presently beleaguered by charges of a blatant and persistent concealment of widespread paedophilia and sexual abuse, an outcry that has led (amongst others) to the downfall of two former Anglican Archbishops, one of whom was forced to resign soon after being appointed to the highest office in the country.

Cupitt's second concern, human relationships, becomes the means by which he seeks to address the subject of ethics. He argues that a new order of personal relationships is needed, and he looks to Romantics and anarchists to supply inspiration. We fight not for a new creed but to discover a new basis for human relationships. So far, religion may have been disciplinary and repressive, but now there *must* be another form of religion. Citing feminism as one of many forces involved in the revolt against patriarchal rationality, its authority claims, and its hierarchical structures, he envisages the new churches modeled after the postmodern world: "a living horizontal network, a multicellular ferment of communication."[10] The religion of the future is

> dispersing God into people, people into their own communicative activities, and the cosmos into an unceasing, endlessly self-renewing process of communal artistic production. *Our* work of art.[11]

Cupitt reiterates that there is no advantage to be gained by breaking away from ecclesiastical structures. One should try to reinterpret one's own inherited vocabulary within mainstream Christianity rather than in the "thinner and artificial language of some new and smaller group."[12] People might dream of solving the problems of the universe in some group with the supposedly correct creed, but he doubts that there is such a group—or such a creed. And such a dream likely leads to idolatry of the group. Rather, he advocates that we should remain in the Church, but keep our eyes wide open!

That "original vision" was slightly modified in 2001 with his book *Reforming Christianity*. He berates the Church for being "stuck up its own cul-de-sac" unable and unlikely to reform itself; and considers that it is consigning itself to the heritage industry, which will lovingly restore and preserve it, unchanging and dead. He sees the immense progress that has been achieved by those organizations and individuals who are outside the Church, yet influenced by Christian values have championed "human emancipation, human rights (and) humanitarian ethics."[13] This is the reformation of Christianity—a desupernaturalized, secular, Kingdom religion. The crucial point to note is not that humanism has developed out of a reaction to Christianity, but that secular humanism is "Christianity's own struggle to advance from its relatively warped ecclesiastical to its final, 'kingdom,' stage of development."[14] This same idea, as we shall soon see, is also found in the writings of Lloyd Geering. The demise of the Church is not the end of Christianity, for Christianity is still unfolding in secular humanism. What we are now witnessing is a change of dispensation, as the Church's own inner logic brings it to an end and Christianity is metamorphosed into its long-awaited, post-ecclesiastical, Kingdom form. Cupitt can even see small signs that the Church itself has begun to change; he cites the obvious fact that the emphasis in its rites of passage (baptism, confirmation, marriage and death) has shifted from concern with another world to affirming *this life*. The funeral sermon that used to centre on the eternal destiny of the soul of the deceased has given way to a homily that recalls the life of the deceased. The future life is traded for *this* life. Still, the main burden of his argument is that the Church's downfall, although gradual, is inevitable; and he is not too distressed at its passing because Kingdom Christianity is replacing it. He identifies the core teaching of Kingdom Christianity:

- Religious meaning has become dispersed across culture in everyday language and the religious/secular distinction has been erased. The whole of life is religious. (*Life, Life*)
- Life is outsideless and we should commit ourselves unreservedly to our own transient lives. (*Creation out of Nothing*)
- There is no absolute religious object, but there are valid religious attitudes. Salvation is found not by withdrawing from the world, but in expressive, solar living. (*Solar Ethics*)
- Life and death are not polar opposites but are always mingled. Life involves the awareness of the closeness of death. (*Emptiness and Brightness*)
- Humanism and humanitarian ethics are expressions of a new global religious way of life. (*After God, Everyday Speech* books)
- Ecclesiastical Christianity is to be replaced by informal religious associations, which emphasize sharing one's story and Kingdom values. (*Philosophy's own Religion, Reforming Christianity*)[15]

It can be seen, then, that Cupitt's vision of the future faith brings him to a point where he looks *beyond* the churches, a position similar to Spong's idea of the ecclesia of the future. The new note that has been sounded since 2000 is his admission that his writing is "not addressed to the church [but is] for me and others who think as I do."[16] Cupitt thinks that ecclesiastical Christianity will be replaced by informal religious associations and networks. Indeed, it is highly significant to note that in recent years there has been an explosion of loose associations of liberal and radical Christians throughout the Western world. People are moving on from Church Christianity, which is in terminal decline, to the Kingdom religion that secularism and globalization are pointing towards.

Cupitt resembles Spong in yet another way: he, too, proclaims himself to be "post-Christian." By this he means that the religion of the future must be based on the dream of a Kingdom that is *this-worldly*—one that shows the way to religious fulfilment in *this* (and *only this*) life, and that secular culture (much more than the churches) has begun to realize. He demonstrates how that ancient religious dream has been pursued through the United Nations, international law, democratic politics, ceaseless global communication, and humanitarian ethics. The world is now committed to the struggle for the emancipation of women and the reconciliation of ethnic and religious differences. It was left to the secular world, especially in such "events" as Martin Luther King's "I Have a Dream" speech and John Lennon's "Imagine," to tell the story of a "new world" in which people would live together in harmony and hope for a better day would be re-ignited. It is interesting that in the advertising for the Games of the XXVII[th] Olympiad (Sydney, 2000) sport was portrayed as embodying the democratic and communal values that ennobles communities when people of all races, creeds and genders "celebrate humanity." This tallies nicely with Pierre de Coubertin's characterization of the Olympics as "humanity's superior religion."

Cupitt's opponents, especially John Milbank and others of the "radical orthodox" school of theologians, regard his views as an unmitigated nihilism that can be rescued only by theology. On the contrary, declares Cupitt, what they mistakenly brand as nihilism is ethical humanitarianism that cares for others solely on the basis of our co-humanity "regardless of race, colour, creed, gender, sexual orientation, doctrinal soundness and moral desert."[17] Unlike radical orthodoxy and conservative religion, both of which reinforce anachronistic distinctions between God and human, master and servant, light and darkness, the "nihilistic" vision sees a world in which everything is on the same level, open and explicit. This is also the Kingdom vision of postmodern secularism—and of early Christianity. This "new world" represents a much more accurate and nuanced version of the original Christian programme than anything available from the churches.

To summarize: Cupitt's reformation of Christianity has progressed from desupernaturalising ecclesiastical theology (the original vision) to realizing the ethical message of Jesus in creating kingdom religion in the here-and-now. All of us are now called upon to be religious artists, busy at creating a better world in which to live.

It is this latter agenda—creating kingdom religion—that has long been the major concern of New Zealand non-realist, Lloyd Geering. Geering is often referred to as "the Don Cupitt of New Zealand," but that distorts the unique contribution that he has made in advancing new ideas about the faith of the future. In fact, Geering began writing at least a decade before Cupitt and quite independently of him, and arrived in *Faith's New Age* at almost the same conclusions as those Cupitt announced in *Taking Leave of God*. Perhaps we should refer to Cupitt as "the Geering of the United Kingdom." In some ways he has been even more of a pioneer than Cupitt, for he has been developing his own global vision of the religion of the future since the 1970s. His non-realism finds its expression in the hope for the emergence of a unified and fully globalized world and a global human consciousness.

It is fair to say that Geering, much more than Cupitt, tends to be concerned with the specifics of exactly *how* non-realism can be used to connect with the issues that face people day by day. As Special Lecturer for the St. Andrew's Trust for the Study of Religion and Society, he has done much to increase the religious literacy of the general public by publishing a host of booklets on topical religious themes. These have included, *Images of the City* (1984); *Science, Religion and Technology* (1985); *Machines, Computers and People* (1986); *Encounters with Evil* (1986); *On Becoming Human* (1988); *Creating the New Ethic* (1991); *God and the New Physics* (1995); *New Idols for Old* (1997); *Fundamentalism: The Challenge to the Secular World* (2003); *Is Christianity Going Anywhere?* (2004); and *The Greening of Christianity* (2005).

Just how does Geering propose to redefine Christianity? In order to understand his reasoning one must incorporate shifts in meaning of two words: religion and secular.

In redefining the word "religion" Geering appropriates the ideas of theologian W. Cantwell Smith in his book, *The Meaning and End of Religion*. Here, Smith argued that instead of defining religion as an objective noun to refer to a specific set of beliefs and practices, we should pay attention to *what it means to be religious*. Since many people are religious without belonging to a particular religion, to be religious involves a devoutness or commitment: "a conscientious concern for what really matters"; it means being dedicated to or earnest about a set of guiding principles. Like Spong, Geering adopts Paul Tillich's suggestion that religion is the state of being grasped by an ultimate concern. This way of being religious transcends culture, for even though people from differing cultures might express devotion to God or gods in diverse ways, they share in seeking to answer the question, "What is the meaning of existence?" As Geering observes:

> It was not their belief in the existence of gods which determined how religious they were but the quality of reverence they displayed towards what concerned them ultimately in the world they had constructed.[18]

For Geering, to be truly religious in today's world is to change the content of the God-symbol. Whereas in times past the god-symbol might have been used to assure the preservation of a particular tribe or to defeat of its enemies in battle, today that symbol must be utilized for the preservation of the cosmos. God is now a symbol for what confronts the Universe most urgently—its own destruction:

> If we choose to speak of God, we shall be using this term to focus on all that we supremely value and on the goals which make human existence meaningful and worthwhile; and there is no thing and no place in which we do not encounter this God. . . . This God is in the physical earth of which we are a tiny part. Even more, this God is to be found in all living creatures. Most of all, however, this God is rising to self-awareness in the (as yet) confused collective consciousness of the global human community. This is tomorrow's God, calling us from a world yet to be created. But, to create this world, this God has no hands but our hands, no voice but our voice, no mind but our mind, and no plan for the future except what we plan.[19]

In his book, *The World to Come*, he argues that "a faith for the future" must take into account the frightening scenarios that might befall the world, from thermonuclear holocaust to social and economic chaos. The religion of the future must therefore work towards minimizing such threats. Being religious is being ultimately concerned with pressing issues that confront humankind, among which are the following:

- The human population explosion, which threatens to outstrip our capacity to ensure that all are provided with even the basics for existence
- The rapid exhaustion of the earth's non-renewable resources
- The increase in pollution that threatens human access to air and water
- The destruction of rain-forests and the increase in desert areas that affects the delicate ecological balance
- The destruction of the ozone layer that results in climatic change and global warming
- The interdependence of nations in the global village—one inappropriate choice by one nation affects another[20]

Geering thus shares the concerns of a growing number of theologians and scientists such as Anne Primavesi and Ursula Goodenough that ecological issues demand a religious response. Indeed, even a non-theist like Goodenough admits that the need for a planetary ethic in response to global self-destruction is a religious reaction. In her book, *The Sacred Depths of Nature,* she echoes Geering:

> That we need a planetary ethic is so obvious that I need but list a few key words: climate, ethnic cleansing, fossil fuels, habitat preservation, human rights, hunger, infectious disease, nuclear weapons, oceans, ozone layer,

pollution, population. Our global conversations on these topics are, by definition, cacophonies of national, cultural and religious self-interest. Without a common religious orientation, we don't basically know where to begin, nor do we know what to say or how to listen, nor are we motivated to respond.[21]

Having come to understand religion anew, Geering proposes, we need to redefine what we mean by the word secular. For him secularism is not, as usually portrayed, the opposite of being religious. Rather, it is his contention that secularism has evolved out of Christianity in the same way that Christianity evolved out of Judaism. The Enlightenment project in the nineteenth century is not a curse as so many conservative theologians like Alistair MacIntyre assert, but provided the necessary spur to develop such concepts as humanism and ethical humanitarianism. New freedoms and social changes brought liberation. The divine right of kings was replaced by democracy, slaves were emancipated, colonies became self-governing countries, discrimination due to gender, sexual orientation and ethnicity was outlawed. The freedom to think, act and explore ideas is enshrined in our secular, humanistic culture. For Geering this secular world has evolved out of the Western Christian culture and in particular from the life and teachings of Jesus of Nazareth. Geering endorses Albert Loisy's observation that "Jesus preached the Kingdom, but it was the Church who came." Jesus' message was not aimed at a supernatural Kingdom in the next world, but a Kingdom (or realm) of human justice and equality here and now. Endorsing the conclusions of the Jesus Seminar, he views Jesus as a "man of wisdom par excellence" and "a secular sage (who) obliterates the boundaries separating the sacred from the secular," arguing that much of what Jesus spoke about in terms of the kingdom is already being realized by secular society, though there is still much work to be done to complete the task.[22] In *Christianity without God* he celebrates the secular humanism that appropriates from the Jesus story the idea of the Kingdom —once seen as a theological concept, but today best described as a new global and ecological world that we urgently need to establish. Geering thus combines his non-realism with the historical research of the Jesus Seminar in arguing for a non-realist interpretation of the Christian story, a rendering that celebrates humanity and the potential for a new heaven and a new earth in this world. It is a bold project that broadens the parameters set by Cupitt.

To summarize, then, both Cupitt and Geering want to throw away the former distinction between the natural order and the supernatural realm. They advocate learning instead to see the world, and within it our own life, as one continuous flowing, evolving process. There is only this world, and how we respond to the encompassing threats to ourselves on a personal and global level is what makes us religious. To use the word "God" is to say something profound about what most affects us—our Ultimate concern. This is the non-realist outlook. Whilst Cupitt's emphasis is more upon the individual getting him/herself together and making sense of the human condition, Geering seeks to engage a unified and global world in an effort to break down tribalism and ethnicity. These interrelated emphases are two halves of the whole—the self and the world, an all-encompassing combination indeed worthy of ultimate concern. Put quite simply, non-realism is aimed at getting ourselves and our planet in shape to tackle what life throws at us so that we can preserve and extend the world we inhabit. This is the task of religion!

# 4

## THE SPIRITUALITY REVOLUTION
## GRASSROOTS SPIRITUALITY

In the 1950s and '60s social scientists promoted what became known as "the secularization theory."[1] Simply put, it was the notion that modernization would lead to a decline of religion in both society and in the minds of individuals. It was commonly assumed that as the effects of the Enlightenment increasingly took hold, people would lose their religious beliefs and become ever more secular. But even one of the main proponents of secularization theory, Peter Berger, now admits that the theory was flawed:

> The assumption that we live in a secularized world is false. The world today, with some exceptions . . . is as furiously religious as it ever was, and in some places more so than ever. This means that a whole body of literature by historians loosely labelled "secularization theory" is essentially mistaken.[2]

Berger points to the powerful movement of counter-secularization that, as I noted in chapter 1, is clearly at work in conservative versions of Islam and Christianity. But this is only one part of the picture of the resurgence of interest in religion. Another large religious movement tends to be overlooked or ignored by social analysts who find religious fundamentalism a more provocative topic. Religious ambiguity resulting from recent shifts in the nature of religious belief and praxis across the world has given rise to the myriad "alternative spiritualities" that now dot the religious landscape. Not only does this populist groundswell defy traditional forms of religious categorization, but alternative spiritualities have made it increasingly difficult to define "mainstream religion." To dismiss religious experimentation and the personal customization of spirituality from various sources as "deviant" is no longer appropriate. Even in America, where fundamentalist religion supposedly goes hand in hand with political ideology, one finds many whose religious identity is difficult to categorize:

> The Bush administration's dance with religion doesn't have much of a partner in the Pacific Northwest (of America). This is the least religious part of the country. Ask people here, "What's your religion?" and twenty-five percent say, "I don't have one." Almost sixty-three percent don't belong to a religious community. Nationally, only fourteen percent claim no religion and forty-one percent join no church. . . . (B)ut it's a mistake to see the contest as between believers and heathens. While most people in the Pacific Northwest do without church, they are rarely atheists or agnostics. Even amongst those who said they have no religion, sixty-seven percent believe that God exists.[3]

In this chapter I will argue that we should take seriously those different spiritual voices that are presently competing for followers in the Western religious supermarket. This smorgasbord has often been referred to as "New Age" but that label is often used in a pejorative way by those who, opposed to religious and spiritual experimentation, write from a position of perceived religious supremacy. I prefer the phrase "alternative spiritualities," which acknowledges a spiritual search that is wide-ranging and dynamic. People in the Western world are not irreligious; on the contrary, many have become even more religious—or, as the current terminology expresses it, "they are spiritual." The shift from religion to spirituality is evident in the increasingly heard phrase, "I'm not religious, but I am spiritual." Simply put, the "death of God" and the resulting secularization of society have not reduced the number of spiritual options, but rather resulted in their proliferation. This rise in spirituality is confirmed by research conducted in America, Australia and Europe.

In America Robert Forman of the Forge Institute broadens the definition of the second axial age to include a new form of spirituality that is "focused on the personal, experiential and transcendental" and is "populist, disorganized, yet potentially greater numerically than some of the existing world religions." He calls this "grassroots spirituality." Here are some of his facts and figures:

- Between one half and one third of Americans report a 'spiritual experience' that has had a significant impact upon their lives.[4]
- 23% regularly do yoga or meditation.
- 40% of those who call themselves 'religious' do not belong to church, mosque or synagogue.
- 1,158,850 people belong to AA (Alcoholics Anonymous) or a similarly spiritual group and five million have participated in 12-step programmes (ALANON, OA, SA, etc.).
- Some three million spiritual groups are presently active.
- Many non-fiction books about spirituality—for example, *The Road Less Traveled*, *Care of the Soul* and *Chicken Soup for the Soul*—have been at the top of *The New York Times* bestseller list.

Whilst most attention in the religious press has naturally centred on the rise of fundamentalism—due either to its political sympathies or its link with terrorism—Forman's research points us in another direction: the rise of popular spirituality. It is a striking paradox that while mainstream Christian denominations in the West are declining at a rate of over twenty percent per decade and fundamentalist religious groups respond with apocalyptic anger, the thirst for alternative spiritualities and meditative techniques has never been greater. Driven by people at the grassroots, an ever-growing expansion of the spiritual marketplace has resulted in an abandonment of hierarchy and the priestly class and a diminished dependency on institutional forms. People are happy to network, to gather occasionally and accommodate their spirituality to their other life-concerns:

> This spiritual movement is burgeoning mostly on the margins of mainstream, popular culture and traditional church hierarchies. It is growing not in science labs, parish naves or university classrooms, but rather in living rooms, church basements, yoga centers, nature walks, meditation rooms and coffee shops all over the nation and world. It is at heart populist, devoid of leadership or overarching organization.[5]

That situation is repeated in Australia, a country that is said to be "the most irreligious place on earth." The Australian sociologist David Tacey argues in a series of books (*Edge of the Sacred, ReEnchantment, The Spirituality Revolution*) that "a spirituality revolution" is taking place today. It is being fuelled by ordinary folk who are moving away from the historic religions and forging a multitude of spiritual paths. It seems that people are creative religious performers with a corresponding array of "artistic" spiritualities helping to guide them through life.

In a very revealing anecdote in *ReEnchantment*, Tacey notes that a minister who had read his first book, *Edge of the Sacred*, telephoned to enquire why the new spirituality in Australia did not mean an increase in the number of people attending mainstream churches.[6] The questioner's unspoken assumption—that the churches still have a monopoly on spirituality and people will go there first for spiritual nourishment—showed how little understanding even the clergy have about the spiritual/religious preferences of the vast majority of the population. People in Australia are opting for what I would describe as a "smorgasbord of therapeutic spiritualities." Spiritual preferences (note the plural) are chosen by participants to aid their own personal well-being. Apparently people select their spiritualities in much the same way they would choose from the wide variety of dishes one finds on a smorgasbord in a restaurant. If it has a pleasing taste and promotes good health and well-being, then they will buy it. If it works (that is, if it has therapeutic value) then they will use it. If it doesn't work then they will discard it and try another brand. This is a consumer-driven market. Moreover, it is not a matter of buying only one product. The contours of grassroots spirituality become very blurred, as the sociologist Gary Bouma observes:

> Australians are likely to dabble in a wide variety of spiritual activities and not be bothered by what in an earlier time would have been seen as inconsistent or conflicting involvements. I know of Anglicans who consult their horoscopes, Catholics who do Tai Chi, Atheists who wear crosses, Baptists who meditate, Vietnamese immigrants who see no conflict in being Catholic and Buddhist at the same time, and Jews who seriously practice witchcraft. Spirituality has become an area of self-directed and self-assessed activity. No longer are the

norms of an organization attended to if they get in the way. Brand loyalty is in free-fall decline, product sampling is rampant and vast amounts of advice on how to do it are available on the web, in bookstores and newsagents.[7]

For many Australians, then, the spiritual can take place with or without reference to the Christian churches. The former spiritual myopia that presented faith as a Kierkegaardian either/or scenario and resulted in people being restricted to a prescribed fashion has failed. Participants in the spirituality revolution of the New Millennium will not heed the antiquated injunction that "this is the *only* way." The new religious attitude accepts such diverse techniques as labyrinth-walking, meditating, yoga, color or aroma therapy, the Enneagram, Neuro-Linguistic Programming, the Myers-Briggs Type Indicator, spiritual healing, creation and eco-centred spirituality—the list is nearly endless. Moreover, numerous and supposedly "doctrinally orthodox" Christians are participants in this new wave of spiritual enquiry. Many mix this heady spiritual cocktail with the traditional disciplines found in such ancient sources as Benedict, Ignatius and Julian of Norwich. The postmodern return to the third person of the Trinity—the Spirit—represents a new respect for the sacred in everything. And, as we have been assured, the spirit leads wherever it will. Thus it is commonplace for people to "pick and mix" their spiritual paths. Many reject both the churches and secularism by striking out boldly and seeking their own spiritual way from many differing sources, some of which might once have been considered contradictory.

As a result of taking up the reins as Director of Wollaston College in Perth, Western Australia some years ago, I am among those whose eyes have been forcibly opened to what has been happening in the spirituality revolution. This institution, operated by the Anglican Diocese of Perth, was built in the 1950s as a residential theological college for the training of Anglican priests. Due to monetary constraints and a changed ministry model, full-time students are now non-residential and attend the college only one day a week for what is termed "priestly formation." Confronted with the problem of maintaining a thirty-bedroom facility, the Diocese invested heavily to expand the complex with new conference facilities. Overlooking the Indian Ocean and adjoining a national park, it has an ideal location; but who would be interested in what it had to offer? Given the relatively small population of Perth (1.2 million), I have been staggered by the number of spirituality groups that have used our facilities. Here is but a sample: Power Energetics, Shayagriva (Buddhism), Core Energetics, Healing Touch, Innerglow, Infinite Choice, Reiki, Therapeutic Massage, Pilates, Yoga (of many different sorts), Shivalabalayogi, Impersonal Enlightenment Foundation, Siddhayoga, Essential Oils, Sound Healing, Color Therapy, Homeopathy, Creative Dance, Dumiya Meditation, Creative Memories, Sacred Space: Sacred Mind, Conscious Living, Totally Alive, Healing Touch, Sacred Healing, Abdy, Bush Flower Essences, and Mindful Heart: Heartful Mind.

What I have experienced at Wollaston accords with much that Robert Forman writes in *Grassroots Spirituality* and what David Tacey argues is happening in the spirituality revolution. Three quick portraits will give you an inkling of the current spirituality scene.

### PORTRAIT 1

A. is the founder and main practitioner of a spiritual institute called Power Energetics™. Her spirituality is a mixture of yoga with aerobics. She describes it as

> A workout for the soul: a healing journey of Energy Movement and Self Transformation and aligning one's consciousness with an inner presence of Harmony, Power and Vitality. The underlying principle is that everything that has occurred in our existence is stored on an energetic level in and around our body and is explored to its depths. The Power Energetics™ movement exercises encourage and support the body on all levels to release and integrate blocked energy, tension and stress. The Power Energetics™ courses and Energy Fitness classes are designed to move energy, inspire authentic self expression and increase the flow of vital life-force throughout the body on all levels.[8]

Classes of thirty people turn up each week for their "workout for the soul." It is hoped to expand the workshops to all parts of Australia and that it will become mainstream.

### PORTRAIT 2

B. is an ordained minister, employed in a Church school. A few years ago she undertook a 12-step programme. She has two permanent tattoos. On her left shoulder is an angel; on her leg is the Buddhist yin/yang symbol. She wears a stud in her nose. Her sermons for School Chapel are taken from *Chicken Soup for the Soul*. Her Religious Education classes use guided meditation and reflective silence.

### PORTRAIT 3

One of the assignments I set in a Diploma Course on Australian Spirituality and Theology was to research a contemporary spirituality and compare its teachings with the Anglican faith. C's study was especially illuminating in that it is an example of a growing trend towards people belonging to more than one faith community. She is both a Christian and a follower of an international spiritual organization named Subud, founded by an Indonesian Muslim in the 1950s. Following the apophatic tradition, Subuds believe that God is Ultimate mystery, but by using the prescribed meditative techniques we can be the recipients of God's grace. Interestingly, C. described it as experiencing what Paul Tillich calls "the Ground of Our Being." Subud defines itself not as a religion, but as a practice. It has no clergy and is bound by few rules and dogmas. This non-hierarchical, democratic group encourages people not to see Subud as *the* religion, but also to be members of main-stream faiths in whichever country they live. Thus they combine a sense of the Ultimate mystery of life with being part of a larger worshipping community that may experience God through Christ or Allah in the teachings of Muhammad. Urged by other Subud members to belong to a mainstream religious tradition, my student was baptized as an Anglican three years ago. She finds no contradiction in being both an Anglican and a Subud.[9]

The growing influence of alternative spiritualities is similar in Europe, where in the last hundred years traditional institutional Christianity has shown a precipitate decline. In the publication, *Gone but not Forgotten*, Philip Richter and Leslie Francis have categorized the people of the United Kingdom into five groups according to their allegiance to the Church: "regular attenders," "fringe attenders," "open de-churched," "closed de-churched" and "non-churched." Across the denominational spectrum, only ten percent of the population attend their church regularly, that is, five to eight times in a two-month period. Similarly there are ten percent fringe attenders who go to church one to three times in a two-month period. Significantly, however, forty percent of the population are "de-churched," meaning that at some point in their life they attended church but do no longer. Of these, twenty percent are the "open de-churched"—people who are open to return if suitably contacted and invited—and twenty are "closed de-churched": those who were somehow harmed or disillusioned and have no intention of returning. The remaining forty percent of the population nationally are non-churched, never having been to church, except perhaps for the funeral or wedding of a friend or relation.[10] It can be seen from these results that the decline in church allegiance is well advanced, inasmuch as sixty percent of the population have no contact with the Church and are unlikely to do so in the future.

Grace Davie, who similarly finds that Western Europeans are now unchurched populations, contends that their lack of allegiance to the churches does not mean that people have embraced secularism *in toto*; rather she describes them as "believing without belonging." Europeans might have left the churches and chapels, but that does not mean that they have "yet abandoned many of their deep-seated religious inclinations."[11] Indeed, she asserts that Europe's declining church membership and attendance is the exception to the general thrust of the rest of the world who are becoming more churched, especially in the United States of America. However, she does admit that the drift from institutional Christianity in Europe has meant that people's beliefs have become less orthodox. Without the churches' policing and reinforcement, people both "forget the details" of their faith and are open to all kinds of different religious messages. This is corroborated by evidence from research undertaken in the United Kingdom:

> Study after study appears to prove that people are increasingly losing faith in the Church and the Bible and turning instead to mysticism in guises ranging

from astrology to reiki and holistic healing. . . . More and more people describe themselves as spiritual, fewer as religious and, as they do so they are turning away from the Christian Church. . . . Twice as many people believe in a "spirit force" within than they do an Almighty God without.[12]

In their book *The Spiritual Revolution*, Linda Woodhead and Paul Heelas argue that Christianity will be eclipsed by spirituality in the United Kingdom within the next twenty to thirty years and that this movement will prove more significant than the Protestant Reformation of the sixteenth century. Their findings are based on research conducted in Kendal, a typically conservative British town with a population of 28,000, in which they measured the growth of the "holistic milieu"—which one might also term "alternative spiritualities"—and the decline of Christian congregational worship. Although these new forms hardly constitute a mainstream phenomenon (less than two percent of the population nationally participate), their explosive rate of growth among not only the young but also the middle-aged and even elderly is a threat to traditional churchgoing. Indeed, this study found that Kendal mirrors the national statistics with eerie precision: 2,207 people in the town (7.9 percent of the local population) attend church on Sunday, while 600 (1.6 percent) take part in some kind of holistic activity. During the 1990s, when the town's population grew by 11.4 percent, participation in the "new spirituality" grew by 300 percent.

Woodhead and Heelas contend that "mini revolutions" have already taken place, and point out that in Kendal the holistic milieu now outnumbers every single major denomination apart from Anglicans. They estimate that if the holistic milieu continues the linear growth it has shown since 1970, and if the congregational domain continues to decline at the same rate over the same period, then the spiritual revolution will take place during the third decade of the third millennium. Interestingly, they also echo Don Cupitt's argument that ordinary language reflects current religious belief, pointing to the currency of once specifically religious terms such as "feng shui" and "yin and yang" that are now elements of common parlance. By contrast, theistic language has lost its vitality in ordinary language: "goodbye", for instance, no longer means "God be with you." The way that religious ideas have been taken over by ordinary language reveals the lessening of the authority of the churches and the social empowerment of individuals in modern times. A symbol of this spiritual revolution is neatly expressed in the fate of one of the local churches:

> If you were searching for a symbol of this revolution, you need look no further than the United Reformed Church in Dent. This building was once the nucleus of the Christian community of Dent, a quintessentially English village a few miles outside Kendal. But over the years apathy crept in and the congregation declined until it was down to one. To raise money, the church hired out its old schoolroom as a spiritual meditation centre. Local interest in meditation

ballooned. When the church was forced to sell the building the meditation group bought it and refurbished it. Now it is flourishing where the old church failed. One of its trustees is a Church of England warden.[13]

Before attempting a final evaluation of this evidence from America, Australia and Europe, it may be a reasonable caution to include the insights of the sociologist of religion, Steve Bruce. In his book, *God Is Dead: Secularization in the West* he reaffirms the secularization theory. Although he does not view the collapse of belief as imminent, nevertheless the "long term decline in the power, popularity and prestige of religious beliefs and rituals" is inevitable.[14] He also argues that we should beware of jumping to hasty conclusions as to the effect of alternative spiritualities. He cautions (as revealed by Woodhead and Heelas too) that the overall numbers interested in alternative spirituality are not as large as often portrayed and that people have not necessarily left the church specifically in order to join alternative spiritualities. Indeed, he estimates that the number of spiritual seekers would do no more than "fill the space left by the decline of just one denomination."[15] Moreover, he suspects that these differing spiritualities lack the "detailed agreement on substance to create a cultural movement with momentum."[16] With an emphasis upon individualism and "just making you better at what you are *already* doing" they lack core objectives that could unite them in a common project. For Bruce, alternative spiritualities are too diverse and focused on the individual to provide the cohesiveness necessary for a collective impact. With as many definitions of what it means to be spiritual as there are spiritual people, this "movement" will never provide a sustained challenge to either the churches or secularism.

It is here that Forman finds an answer to Bruce and those who doubt whether alternative spiritualities share any unifying element. Forman identifies belief in "God" as that which unites those involved in grassroots spirituality, though this definition includes those for whom God is a non-personal "universal energy or spirit." His central thesis is that grassroots spirituality involves a vaguely panentheist ultimate that

> is indwelling, sometimes bodily, as the deepest self *and* accessed through not-strictly-rational means *of* self-transformation and group process *that* becomes the holistic organisation for all life.[17]

Let me examine this definition. First, it is called "grassroots" because it has developed in a spontaneous and disorganized way among many ordinary people. Its many sources have inspired its different manifestations. No single person or group is in charge, and no overarching organization or hierarchy exists. As I have indicated, it is a broad umbrella, covering diverse groups with highly permeable borders and representing complex and sometimes mutually inconsistent beliefs. A noteworthy and important innovation is that many are teaching others, with spiritual leaders now being described as "facilitators," "spiritual mentors," or "spiritual friends." This sense of shared spiritual journey is reflected in the oft-heard words, "we are all on a common pilgrimage and we are all learning together." Moreover, people frame all aspects of the human condition in spiritual terms—anything from eating disorders to the psychology of the mind. Forman contends that it may be the first "religious-like system" that lacks the overarching leadership of a Gautama, Jesus, or Mohammed.

Second, grassroots spirituality involves belief in a panentheist ultimate that is "indwelling, sometimes bodily, as the deepest self." What this means is that everyone and everything is part of one single principle or essence, but the One is not limited to those worldly phenomena. Thus the panentheism that we encountered in chapter 2 and is associated with the writings of John Spong is enlarged by Forman to include a wide variety of beliefs in a greater 'power' that is also indwelling—anything from 'energy' to 'prana' to 'true nature.' Spong's "God-presence" becomes all embracing and is reflected in the key phrases of grassroots spirituality: "connection to whole/all," "divine energy flowing in us and through us," "God's presence is everywhere," "one in whom we move and live and have our being," "Christ/God consciousness," "relational," and "unity with all things." The idea of a supernatural, transcendent deity is replaced by the belief that we are all interconnected by and with the divine principle. A corresponding resurgence of interest in mysticism has been matched by a suspicion of religious dogma.

Accordingly, we must now direct our attention to exploring spirituality that lies *within* the self rather than outside it. This emphasis upon an imminent conception of the divine is corroborated by Heelas:

> This is the spirituality which is integral to what it is to be truly oneself; which is integral to the natural order as a whole. This is the spirituality which serves as the font of wisdom and judgement, rejecting authoritative sources emanating from some transcendent, tradition-articulated source. This is the spirituality which informs ('expressive') authenticity, creativity, love, vitality. This is the spirituality which interconnects.[18]

This spirituality is obviously indebted to ideas expressed by depth psychologists like C. G. Jung. It further contributes to the weakening of the role of clergy, for people who believe themselves gifted with an indwelling spark of the Divine have no need for a mediating figure like a priest—though they might seek the services of a therapist or counsellor to help discover and analyze a deeper, inner self.

Third, grassroots spirituality is "accessed through . . . self-transformation and group process *that* becomes the holistic organization for all life." By this Forman means that although the indwelling Infinite is veiled from us, we can by a process of inner transformation discover it. The keywords are inner growth, therapy, meditation, ongoing and open ended growth; a process of discovering, journey, process of unfolding, awakening and centring. It is here that there are generally murmurs of disapproval about alternative spiritualities with detractors deriding it as narcissistic and self-centred individualism. Indeed, Jeremy Carrette and Richard King in their book, *Selling Spirituality*, go much further than most, arguing that the takeover of religion by spirituality is supported and even encouraged by capitalism. The increasing privatization of religion (now spirituality) since the Enlightenment is due to the influence of neoliberalism—the belief that life is determined by economic forces alone. Spirituality becomes a useful tool in the promotion of capitalist globalization in that beliefs are seen purely in term of a private, personal choice and are like any other commodity that can be bought and sold in the marketplace. Consequently one of the important traditional roles of religion in providing a counter-ethical perspective and thus correcting the abuses of governments is curbed. People now can follow their own spiritual path without critiquing the ethics/morality of their political situation. According to Carrette and King what is needed is a "counter-discourse, grounded in an emphasis upon social justice and compassion to displace the privatized and neoliberal framing of spirituality."[19] Whilst I would concur with Carrette and King that some spiritualities are guilty of being commercially driven, it seems far-fetched to argue that capitalism is the *prime mover* in the rise of spirituality. As I have shown in this chapter there are many varied factors that have contributed to the decline of religion and the emergence of the spiritual revolution. Likewise, many traditional religions, especially in the United States of America, have prostrated themselves before the altar of capitalism. Religion *per se* is no guarantee against the excesses of capitalism. Indeed, it is true to say that historically there has often been a reciprocal relationship of missionary activity and colonial expansionism, as indicated in the celebrated remark of Archbishop Desmond Tutu:

> When the white man arrived we had plenty of land and he had the Bible. . . . [Then] the white man taught us to pray, and when we opened our eyes, we had the Bible and he had the land.[20]

Both religions and spiritualities alike are guilty of ignoring issues of justice and equality. Moreover, whilst the excesses of the capitalist system must always be criticized and the system needs continual reform, it is fair to say that capitalism also contains within it an effective system of social and economic polity.

I would thus argue that this dismissive labelling of grassroots spirituality ignores the communal aspect of the new spiritual search. To be sure, it can be conducted in isolation, but more often than not it occurs in small "intimate" groups. People want to journey with others undertaking a *shared* pilgrimage—not necessarily with the person who lives next door or in the same city, but rather in the company of those who are fellow spiritual seekers. Likewise, they have made use of the communication superhighway—the internet—and established "virtual" spiritual societies in cyberspace. Moreover, one finds people prepared to travel, sometimes long-distances, to attend conferences, workshops and retreats with like-minded participants. People are creating spiritual communities of care that transcend geographical and even national boundaries. As Woodhead remarks:

> I would say it is inaccurate to say that people are doing this just for pleasure. Trying to become yourself but better through your relationships with others is a very noble activity.[21]

In order for spirituality to be complete it must eventually guide the whole of one's life and it must in some way change the life of the practitioner for the better. Grassroots spirituality is much more than pampering the self in a spa-bath full of bushflower essences.

To conclude, it may be argued that whilst grassroots spirituality is not at the moment as large as the churches it has the *potential* to be numerically greater than any of the existing religious institutions. Although as Forman admits, it lacks the organizational structure to provide social cohesion, it tends to attract financially comfortable and well-educated people who, once economic survival requirements are met, shift into concerns to the "higher order" needs of the self. Simply put, the more materially affluent, the more likely one is to have the time and resources to explore one's spirituality. The theological outlook is henotheistic in that people in grassroots spirituality are religiously tolerant and respectful of other's beliefs; they "all hold [their] version of the infinite to be ultimate without denying the ultimacy of other systems." Significantly, those in grassroots spirituality evince little or no allegiance to the beliefs of their parents, family, peers, or partner because everything centres on choices that "I" make in deciding which spiritual way is best for me. The latest marketing skills are much in evidence, with many dispensers of spirituality being "media savvy" and such notable books as *The Celestine Prophesy, Chicken Soup for the Soul, Be Here Now, Conversations with God* finding their way to the list of all-time best sellers. Interestingly, women are more attracted to grassroots spirituality than men by a ratio of two to one.

Forman's research is echoed by Davie in her insistence that:

> The sacred does not disappear—indeed, in many ways it is becoming more rather than less prevalent in contemporary society.[22]

Likewise Heelas and Woodhead make the intriguing assertion that our present situation is characterized not so much by secularization versus spirituality as the decline in religion viewed as an external, transcendent force and a corresponding rise in spirituality understood as an inner indwelling of the sacred. They invoke what they label "the subjectivization thesis" arguing that people who are concerned about the sacred

> are much more likely to be, or become involved with, those forms which help them cultivate the unique 'irreplaceabilities' of their subjective-lives than those which emphasize the importance of conforming to higher authority.[23]

Simply put, people are replacing one (external/objective) way of understanding the sacred with another (internal/subjective). This conclusion is in turn reinforced by Tacey's observation that in Australia "the one sacred reality manifests itself in different ways to different people . . . the Mysterious One can reveal itself only in and through the Many."[24] Of course, the pluralist paradigm that the sacred can be found through many different manifestations is not a new thesis and has gained considerable support amongst reputable scholars of religion.

As I mentioned in chapter 2, the most famous proponent of pluralism is John Hick. In books such as *God and the Universe of Faiths* (1973) and *God Has Many Names* (1980) he has argued for a theological Copernican revolution. Just as Copernicus displaced the earth from the centre of the universe when he asserted that it rotated on its axis once daily and travelled around the sun once yearly, so Hick stressed that it is not such earthly founders of the faiths but God who is at the centre of religions. All religions serve and revolve around God, not their historical and culturally-relative religious figureheads. Moreover, belief in God begins with a religious experience of the holy that transcends cultures and faiths. Religious experience is foundational to belief, and the differing manifestations of religions are merely human responses to the one divine Reality.

Hick's thesis was primarily aimed at understanding the inter-relationship between the mainline religions of the world. *What is new today (and perhaps not envisaged by Hick) is the fact that those world religions are now competing with a huge array of local, "home-made" or grassroots spiritualities that likewise seek connectedness with a less transcendent and more immanent, subjective kind of god.* The religious and spiritual backdrop of the world has changed considerably. The implications for Christianity and whether it should in any way endorse these manifold spiritualities and spiritual paths will be discussed in detail in chapter 6. Suffice to say, the spiritual revolution poses difficult questions for traditional Christian congregations. How inclusive and accommodating can the Christian faith become? What is distinctive about Christianity that distinguishes it from the beliefs of those in the spirituality revolution? Does Christianity reject the growing trend towards subjectivism in modern culture and reassert its traditional emphasis upon a supernatural, transcendent authority? Or does it risk becoming irrelevant and obsolete by still peddling a message that is not congruent with the one being promoted in the spirituality market-place?

The dawning of the second axial age—a period when people are rethinking everything—can be summed up as the shift from following the great teachers of the world religions (Confucius, Lao Tse, Gautama, Jesus, Mohammed, et al.) to being confident enough to forge our own spiritual paths and even create our own religions! This newfound self-belief in the competency of human beings to attend to their own spiritual needs weakens the controlling influence of the Christian Church and permits people to redefine both their religion and God. In the next chapter I turn my attention to that growing band of people, especially those devoted to the life sciences and ecology, and those in whom the natural world inspires religious wonder and respect. The worship of God is often replaced by mystical feelings of awe for the cosmos and our inter-relatedness with it. Religious naturalism has become a spiritual path that an increasing number of people now take very seriously.

# 5

## RELIGIOUS NATURALISM
## THE AWE AND WONDER OF NATURE

The capacity of the natural world to inspire a religious response from humans has long been recognized. From the nature mysticism of the ancients to present-day expressions of wonderment at the beauty and ferocity of the natural world, it is clear that humans have always sought to understand their relationship to the cosmos. Indeed, as Don Cupitt points out, even hard-nosed rationalist philosophers have succumbed to having religious feelings for nature:

> (T)he English-speaking philosophers remained "mystical" religious naturalists, religiously in love, like all the British and certainly like me, with Nature . . . even as they were busy transforming the old theological vision of the world into the new "experimental philosophy" (i.e., science). They might or might not break with orthodoxy, and they might even become explicit atheists, but they almost always remain religious in their feeling for . . . Nature.[1]

Nature's ability to stir religious feelings in some of the world's most celebrated philosophers and scientists has important implications for the theme of this book: the "God problem." For many, nature has replaced deity as the object of devotion; the scientist James Lovelock went so far as to confer upon our planet the name of the Greek earth goddess, *Gaia*. He was disturbed that a number of his fellow scientists treated the natural world as merely an object of study, rather than as an interconnected whole that needed to be cared for and respected. He therefore sacralized nature and secularized the goddess by positing the notion that "the earth had developed and continues to maintain a self-regulating environment that sustains life and is itself alive."[2] Thus in the Gaia hypothesis humanity is derived from and dependent upon the earth and the needs of humans must be secondary to those of the planet. Lovelock's insights galvanized the ecological movement, and many of its more outspoken members adopted "Gaia" as a brand name to campaign for a more concerted effort by governments to prevent the annihilation of the planet's life-sustaining resources.

This secularizing of the ancient religious notion of "Mother Earth" brings into focus the way that religious feelings can be aroused by the cosmos. Nature comes to be regarded as "sacred" or "divine" and therefore must be treated with the same reverence we would show towards God. As Paul Collins dramatically puts it,

> If we destroy the world, we destroy not only ourselves but the most important symbol of God that we have.[3]

To be a religious naturalist, then, is to possess and enact a profound respect for the cosmos and our place in it.

It is often presupposed that religious naturalism is the product of the recent postmodern "death of God" thinking. However, as Gregory Spearritt correctly asserts: "a naturalistic understanding of religion . . . has a distinguished history."[4] Spearritt is indebted for his remark to an article by J. Wesley Robbins, "When Christians become Naturalists." Robbins outlines how the American Pragmatists (especially William James, John Dewey, and Richard Rorty) proposed solutions to the problem of combining "belief about the world" (i.e. the disappearance of an objective God in the light of scientific thinking) with living a moral/ethical life.[5] Robbins acknowledges William James' belief in "the Almighty," but notes his insistence that "ideal human values are not dependent on, nor authorized" by God.[6] This idea was expanded further by John Dewey, for whom the word "God" designated "ideal values as they were imaginatively unified in human conduct," irrespective of whether they were "realized" in a supernatural Being. For Dewey, the existence of a supernatural entity was a conceptual issue that is always secondary to the main task of "being religious."

However, not all scientists are persuaded by the redefinition of such words as "God" and "religious." In particular, the evolutionary scientist Richard Dawkins derides the current trend amongst distinguished scientists to regard such emotional responses to the cosmos as awe, wonder, joy, or gratitude as being in any way "religious." He also argues that to redefine God using scientific terminology is disingenuous if only because it is contrary to the way that religious people use the word in everyday speech. Not that Dawkins himself believes in an objective God, but this is part of what I see as a "straw-man" strategy. On the one hand, the popular notion of a supernatural being who interrupts the world's processes to perform miracles on behalf of His believers is one that can be easily discredited. On the other, if the words "God" and "religious" are permitted too many definitions, they become moving targets that are impossible to hit; and as a result Dawkins' promotion of the primacy of evolution and atheism becomes more difficult:

> If you count Einstein and Hawking as religious, if you allow the cosmic awe of Goodenough, Davies, Sagan and me as true religion, then science and religion have indeed merged, especially when you factor in such atheist priests as Don Cupitt and many university chaplains. But if the term religion is allowed such a flabbily elastic definition what word is left for conventional religion, religion as the ordinary person in the pew or on the prayer mat understands it today. . . . If *God* is a synonym for the deepest principles of physics, what word is left for a hypothetical being who answers prayers, intervenes to save cancer patients or

helps evolution over difficult jumps, forgives sins or dies for them? If we are allowed to relabel scientific awe as religious impulse, the case goes through on the nod.[7]

Interestingly, Dewey already had an answer to Dawkins' dismissal of religious naturalism: *contra* Dawkins he distinguished between "a religion"—which involved beliefs about the existence of some such entity or ultimate—and "the religious as a function of experience." To put it another way, Dawkins has forensically adduced the theism of others in an attempt to validate his own atheistic position. Dewey's distinction between the beliefs of religions and someone "being religious" also informs the work of Richard Rorty, who has many affinities with Cupitt. Rorty's "being religious" is to engage in an "imaginative project" which is the creation of an "ideal democratic community." So also for Cupitt (though unlike Rorty's emphasis on writers and film makers, he still needs some of the resources of the "religions" of Christianity and Buddhism) the "religious task" is the same—to create a democratic way of living that is equivalent to the Christian emphasis on "a new heaven and a new earth."[8]

Robbins' article thus reveals that for the last century or so the "American Pragmatists" have been advocating a naturalistic reinterpretation of Christian supernaturalism. While Christian theologians have usually responded to this challenge by reverting to critical realism (Robbins calls it "a reiteration of supernaturalism"), the pragmatist need only reassert the advantages in following religious naturalism. Robbins points to four such important "benefits":

1. Religious faith is relieved of the burden of apologetics concerning the existence of divine beings.
2. Religious convictions no longer need to be considered to be in a separate domain from the rest of human thinking and acting—immune from advances in scientific thinking, for instance.
3. Human capacities and responsibilities are affirmed. There is no waiting for some extra-human entity to bring better conditions.
4. A natural piety is involved. Deweyan religious naturalism sees a sense of connectedness, an interdependence between humanity and "the enveloping world that the imagination feels is a universe." It is opposed to militant atheism where humans live defiantly in a hostile world, as well as to supernaturalism in which this world is merely a stage for the drama of human salvation.[9]

These four benefits connect both with Cupitt's project and the religious naturalism that is now being advocated by one of the world's leading cell biologists—Ursula Goodenough. Her religious naturalism is consistent with these Deweyan benefits as she (1) dispenses with the need for a divine being,

(2) reconciles the current biological understanding of the origins of life and workings of the Universe with spiritual yearnings, (3) creatively searches for a religious response to this situation and, (4) argues that the human and the non-human must share the "sacred planet" together. Goodenough considers that a "religious response" to the complexity of the natural world is justified. Indeed, in what she calls her "credo of continuation," she defines herself as a religious naturalist:

> I profess my Faith. For me, the existence of all this complexity and awareness and intent and beauty, and my ability to apprehend it, serves as the ultimate meaning and the ultimate value. The continuation of life reaches around, grabs its own tail, and forms a sacred circle that requires no further justification, no Creator, no superordinate meaning of meaning, no purpose other than that the continuation continue until the sun collapses or the final meteor collides. I confess a credo of continuation.[10]

This statement of faith in *The Sacred Depths of Nature* builds on two earlier articles in the journal of science and religion, *Zygon*, in which she addresses physicist Steven Weinberg's challenge that "the more the universe seems comprehensible, the more it also seems pointless."[11] Goodenough's response to this "nihilistic proposition" is to synthesize the scientific and the religious perspectives. She thus dismisses the principle of "non-overlapping *magisteria*" now in vogue in the science/religion debate and recently championed by the late Stephen Jay Gould in *Rocks of Ages: Science and Religion in the Fullness of Life*. For Gould, there can be no synthesis of religion and science, since each operates in a different domain of authority (*magisterium*)—science in the empirical realm, and religion in the "realm of human purposes, meaning and values."[12] Gould, an agnostic Jew, acknowledges the value and place of religion and even advocates a "respectful [and] loving concordat between the *magisteria* of science and religion."[13] However, whilst meaningful dialogue may be a hoped-for ideal, the reality of a separation of the *magisteria* means that people "must live the fullness of a complete life in many mansions."[14] Gould seems to have employed the non-overlapping *magisteria* approach primarily to combat Creationism and its associated attempts to disguise religion as science. A negative effect, however, was to foster hostility between those representing the two *magisteria* and thus create further competition between science and religion—or as in the case of Richard Dawkins, the conclusion that *only* the scientific approach has real validity. In a two-*magisteria* world, the conflict between science and religion results in scientific reductionism and the unwillingness of those like Dawkins to concede that scientists may have religious feelings.

Goodenough avoids this reductionism by taking the position that she and other non-theistic scientists have good reason to adopt a religious perspective. Indeed, the biological narrative presented by scientists as inherent in the evolution of the world and its species elicits from many observers responses of an undeniably religious nature.[15] Thus Goodenough not only links religious feelings and experience to the natural world, but very significantly links human beings to nature. Avoiding the anthropocentrism of much scientific thinking, she argues that many discoveries in biology reveal that "concepts central to religious thought . . . are in fact operant throughout the biological world."[16] In *The Sacred Depths of Nature* she identifies four religious "principles" implicit in the current biological story of the "Epic of Evolution":

- Ultimacy —asking why things are as they are and why we exist
- Gratitude
- Reverence
- Credo of Continuation (quoted above)

These four religious principles form the basis of a religious naturalism that can inspire people to create a much needed planetary ethic:

> I am convinced that the project (planetary ethic) can be undertaken only if we all experience a solemn gratitude that we exist at all, share a reverence for how life works, and acknowledge a deep and complex imperative that life continue.[17]

Goodenough, who labels herself "an earth-cult evangelist," hopes to instil in others an appreciation of the "beauty" and "mythic potential" of cells and molecules, and offer a "global religious myth."[18] Her writings thus mirror those of Lloyd Geering's ecological concerns in his book *The World to Come*.[19] However, Goodenough also considers two existential problems that have preoccupied Don Cupitt—the fear arising from nihilism, and the facticity of one's own death.

In her first set of reflections Goodenough recounts how at the age of twenty, on a camping trip in Colorado, she looked up into the night sky and was overcome with nihilistic despondency:

> Each star is dying. . . . Our sun too will die, frying the Earth to a crisp during its heat-death, spewing its bits and pieces out into the frigid nothingness of curved spacetime. . . . I wept into my pillow, the long slow tears of adolescent despair. . . . A bleak emptiness overtook me whenever I thought about what was really going on out in the cosmos or deep in the atom.[20]

Goodenough's response to the encroaching nihilism is to admit that she doesn't have to find a "point" to existence and that nature is "a strange but wondrous given."[21] This "epiphany" leads to the opposite of despair—religious awe. In a remarkable passage she describes her religious naturalism:

> I lie on my back under the stars and the unseen galaxies and I let their enormity wash over me. I assimilate the vastness of the distances, the impermanence, the *fact* of it all. I go all the way out and then I go all the way down, to the fact of photons without mass and gauge bosons that become massless at high

temperatures, I take in the abstractions about forces and symmetries and they caress me, like Gregorian chants.[22]

Likewise, her reflections on "multicellularity and death" reveal "one of the central ironies of human existence":

> Our sentient brains are uniquely capable of experiencing deep regret and sorrow and fear at the prospect of our own death, yet it was the invention of death, the invention of the germ/soma dichotomy, that made possible the existence of our brains.[23]

What Goodenough points to is the fact that death is programmed into the "life cycle" of all multicellular organisms. Moreover, "all multicellular organisms are sexual" and thus:

> Sex without death gets you single-celled algae and fungi; sex with a mortal soma gets you the rest of the eukaryotic creatures. Death is the price paid to have trees and clams and birds and grasshoppers, and death is the price paid to have human consciousness, to be aware of all that shimmering awareness and all that love.[24]

No longer is death the cause of anxiety, but now it is the source of a religious experience and she can proclaim, "My somatic life is the wondrous gift wrought by my forthcoming death."[25] Goodenough's religious naturalism is thus very close to Don Cupitt's concern to commit oneself to a religious or "solar" affirmation of life even in the face of death. It also connects with an often overlooked and perhaps surprising facet of Cupitt's writings—his insistence on the value of religious experiences.

Almost alone amongst contemporary radical theologians, Cupitt acknowledges having had religious experiences "every few years since early childhood."[26] Adopting Abraham Maslow's phrase, he lists and explores these "peak experiences" in a chapter entitled "Bliss" in *The Revelation of Being*. He distinguishes between "linguistic" and "visual" experiences. The former are the "religious excitement" that he has encountered when caught up in analyzing certain words, phrases or metaphors. The latter, considerably more intense, include one that occurred in July 1997 as he sat in his study in Emmanuel College, Cambridge and looked out across the broad panorama of Parker's Piece at moving clouds, kites, cars, groups of walkers, and cyclists:

> There was an instant like the moment when a tightly-coiled spring begins to release its energy, and then a violent explosion of pure happiness which passed so rapidly that I became conscious of it and identified it only as something that was already fast receding and becoming forgotten.[27]

Cupitt variously describes this "explosion of pure happiness" as "living outsidelessly," "ecstatic immanence," "the mysticism of secondariness," "Being" or "entostasy." What Cupitt means by these phrases is that this sort of experience compels us to embrace wholeheartedly the natural world with which we human beings are inextricably bound up. The lesson he sees is that people should not attribute such experiences to the working of someone or something outside of themselves—an objective God—but to "the quite-unfathomable continual silent outpouring of everything."[28] Cupitt describes this religious experience as "ineffable," no doubt akin to what Goodenough describes as her "covenant with mystery." Whether one prefers "mystery" or "ineffable," the referent is not a greater being called God, but something (as yet) unknown by scientific enquiry (Goodenough) or the "unthing that is prior to language" (Cupitt). The language of science and the language of philosophy simply assert that the interconnectedness of everything in the cosmos elicits a religious response. Goodenough exclaims, "Hosannah! Not in the highest, but right here, right now, this." Cupitt echoes, "It is eternal happiness, briefly, in and *with* the here and now."[29]

Like Cupitt, Goodenough finds her reflections rising out of her "religion of origin"—Christianity.[30] Using the metaphor of weaving, she binds together (the etymological meaning of religion—*religio*) her scientific story (the "Epic of Evolution") and the Christian story. The tapestry-maker first strings the warp (the Epic of Evolution) and then interweaves the weft (the traditional texts of one's religion of origin). The warp and the weft together make religious naturalism:

> The Epic of Evolution is our warp, destined to endure, commanding our universal gratitude and reverence and commitment. And then, after that, we are all free to be artists, to render in language and painting and song and dance our ultimate hopes and concerns and understandings of human nature.[31]

This commitment to be "artists" echoes Cupitt's plea for individuals to realize themselves through expressive activity and religions to reinvent themselves in the light of the latest advances in scientific thinking. In particular, Goodenough's insistence that the Universe inspires new non-theist religious myths is shared by Cupitt in his love of a "Be-ing" that commands religious respect.[32]

Of course, such a view of the Universe without the underpinning of an objective God does not impress critics like Stephen Webb:

> How this bleak view of relentless fecundity crawling toward final annihilation is sacred is beyond me.[33]

But then, Webb refuses to consider that far from leading to despair, religious naturalism confronts people with the fact that *this world* is the sole source of meaning. It offers no escape to an imagined "Beyond" or "Outside," and one must rather learn to love the transient just as one formerly loved an objective (though to be sure, hypothetical) God.[34] One is led by the following description of the connectedness of humans with nature to suspect that such a religious naturalism has already taken firm root in Australia:

Slowly I begin the final metamorphosis. I must drive out my old self and let the universe in. The creatures will come back not as gods transmogrified, but as themselves. Beaked, furred, fanged, tusked, clawed, hoofed, snouted, they will settle in us, re-entering their old lives deep in our consciousness. And after them the plants themselves. Then we shall begin to take back into ourselves the lakes, the rivers, the oceans of the earth, its plains, its forested crags with their heaps of snow. Then little by little, the firmament, the spirit of things will migrate back into us. We shall be whole.[35]

David Malouf's description of the interconnectedness of human beings and nature is not a new idea, but one that the indigenous people of Australian have been advocating all through their long history. Aborigines recognize no Western dichotomy of spirit/matter or soul/body, but spirit is immanent in body. By this Aboriginal people bear witness to an affiliation with their (sacred) land that can be described only in religious terminology:

In Australian Aboriginal religions the particular land sites are the mediators of vitalistic power (a kind of *élan vital*) if they are cared for and approached in the appropriate way. . . . Aboriginal religions are "geosophical" in that spiritual power and wisdom is linked to places. . . . [So] religious identity is more a question of geography than theology.[36]

This sense of spiritual interconnectedness has been expressed by non-indigenous Australians not in their sense of the land so much as that of the sea. The historical settlement of most "latecomers" in Australia has been at the edge, by the sea. The reasons for the decision of "new invaders" to live close to the sea are fairly obvious—cultural, economic and pragmatic. Moreover, the latest research reveals that 71 percent of those Australians interviewed responded that they "often found a sense of peace and well-being *by the sea*" compared with 28 percent who "often found a sense of peace and well-being *in church*."[37] Perhaps, as the West Australian writer Tim Winton has argued, the sea possesses religious significance for non-indigenous Australians:

The desert is a spiritual place, but we are coastal people, a people who predominantly dwell on our continent's edge. It is there on the beach or pretty near it that the majority of Australians have discovered many things about life and what it means deep down to be Australian . . . The sea is more forthcoming; its miracles and wonders are occasionally more palpable, however inexplicable they be. There is more bounty, more possibility for us in a vista that moves, rolls, surges, twists, rears and changes from minute to minute.[38]

David Malouf similarly observes that if Aborigines are a land-dreaming people, "what we latecomers share is a sea-dreaming, to which the image of Australia as an island has from the beginning been central."[39] Research is currently being undertaken to explore this sea-land division that characterizes Australia's culture.[40] Perhaps it will be shown that it is *not* a case of an either/or, but rather both/and, with both the sea and the land becoming merged in a sense of Aboriginal and non-Aboriginal interconnectedness. If so, people may become more aware of their responsibility to nurture a sustainable ecological environment for all Australians. Indeed, one may argue that this is already beginning to happen, that the burgeoning numbers of bush conservation and beach-care groups indicate how many people are concerned with the protection of the natural environment. And from this it requires but little extrapolation to insist that the future of the planet must be our greatest religious concern.

This point is made most forcefully by Lloyd Geering in *The Greening of Christianity*. Geering's thesis is that an ecological imperative must replace the divine imperative as the basis for ethical action. The planet is in deep crisis with humankind seemingly oblivious to the ecological disaster for which it is responsible. Moreover, the future of humankind is dependent upon the survival of the earth because we have evolved as human beings within the parameters set by the earth's conditions:

> Fascinating though it may be to imagine future space travel to distant stars, it will almost certainly be never more than a delightful fantasy. We are earth creatures, who can live only within the delicately balanced natural forces, geographical conditions and interdependence of species that constitute the ecology of our planetary home. Because of our new understanding of our origins and of the nature of our ecological home, the ethic that concerns us today is no longer the divine imperative but what may be called the Ecological Imperative.[41]

Our focus must change from obeying an external divine imperative (God "out there") to following an internalized earth-centred imperative (God "down here"). We must transfer allegiance from submission to the will of an external divine being to the voicing of our internal religious concerns for the survival of the natural world and its well-being. The fundamental question is no longer "What has God commanded?" but rather "What is good for the planet and all its inhabitants?" Instead of being concerned with our own individual sense of immortality we must be anxious about handing on to the next generation a planet that is fit for human habitation. We must respond to the ecological imperative, not for our own personal benefit, but for those generations yet to come. Indeed, I would suggest that terrorism and fundamentalism, hugely destructive as they may be today, are but minor players on the world stage compared to global warming and the poisoning of the environment. Moreover, humankind's hubris in championing our own importance "above nature," whilst denying the complex interdependence of all things was eloquently expressed by Lewis Thomas over thirty years ago:

> We are told that the trouble with Modern Man [sic] is that he has been trying to detach himself from nature. He sits in the topmost tiers of polymer, glass and steel, dangling his pulsing legs, surveying at a distance the writhing life

of the planet. . . . [However] it is not a new thing for man [sic] to invent an existence that he imagines to be above the rest of life; this has been his most consistent intellectual exertion down the millennia. As illusion, it has never worked out to his satisfaction in the past, any more than it does today. Man [sic] is embedded in nature. The biologic science of recent years has been making this a more urgent fact of life. The new, hard problem will be to cope with the dawning, intensifying realization of just how interlocked we are. The old, clung-to notions most of us have held about our special lordship are being deeply undermined.[42]

In this chapter I have sought to show that for many people respect and concern for the natural world has now replaced devotion to a divine being. In their view, nature should be the object of worship, not God. Indeed, we should love and cherish the earth! If we destroy it, we too are doomed. I have also shown that some of the world's foremost scientists now embrace religious naturalism, and thus demonstrated that nature can inspire religious devotion that is independent of any belief in God. Not only that, but we have seen that religious naturalism has a venerable history, evident in its espousal by American pragmatists. Furthermore, few would deny that religious feelings of awe, wonder gratitude and reverence are appropriate responses to the natural world. Last of all, it has become evident that religious naturalism accurately reflects the spiritual outlook of both indigenous and non-indigenous Australians. One seeker's religious encounter with the Australian landscape provides a moving testament of this faith:

> Several years ago I took a day off from research on wild dolphins to walk miles of remote Australian beach. To the west, the meeting of sea and sky was barely discernible; to the east, searing desert extended 2,000 miles. For hours I walked through this exquisite but barren landscape in utter silence, mourning a recent personal loss. Suddenly, with no warning, the hollow feeling within merged with the emptiness all around into a singular, stunning void that engulfed me with dizzying speed. I collapsed to the ground, reduced to a tiny, isolated speck in a vast, impersonal universe. I struggled to a sitting position, blinking in the midday glare, searching for something, anything, to bring me back to my ordinary self. Nothing. Despite the sun's heat, I felt cold and I was afraid. Then, as if from a great distance, I heard a faint, familiar sound that brought immense relief. A few hundred yards away a dozen cormorants were gathering at the sea's edge to dry their wet, oily wings. . . . Those birds could have been anywhere, but instead by some miracle they were right there, then, with me. I felt wave upon wave of gratitude for their existence and for the existence of all sentient beings.[43]

# 6

## CONCLUSION

In *The Once and Future Faith* Robert Funk sets out the task that confronts those concerned in mapping the future of the Christian faith:

> The future of the Christian faith may turn out to be a minor aspect of the cultural shifts that are shaping our global future. The themes that have dominated the institutional churches may no longer be of central concern to us. But no matter. Yet at the heart of the old faith tradition there are topics and themes that are central to the human condition and the fate of the planet in the next millennium. Our task is to locate those themes and set them in a new and broader context.[1]

In this book I have attempted to delineate what I perceive to be a theme that is central to the human condition—"the God problem"—and set it in a wider context than that envisioned by most Christian theologians. The issue at hand is, after all, much more than an arid debate between atheists and believers.

Although "the God problem" has always been with us and has been expressed by Biblical writers, perhaps most famously the writer of the book of Job, "God" came to be seriously questioned by philosophers beginning with David Hume in the eighteenth century. In his *Dialogues Concerning Natural Religion* Hume made a penetrating philosophical critique of the reasons advanced for belief in God's existence. Whilst Hume is guarded about whether he himself believes in God, his legacy has been to permit his readers to make up their own minds as to the plausibility of belief in God. Of course, the most strident of all attacks on "God" was that of the nineteenth-century German philosopher Friedrich Nietzsche in his parable of the madman in his book, *The Joyous Science*.[2] His pronouncement of the death of God called forth an immediate and still current retort: "This cannot be so!" The sheer existential terror that confronts those who have no supernatural prop on which to rely is too much to bear. The spectre of nihilism (there is No One out there) forces many to insist on the existence of something "more," something greater than we frail and fallible humans, that sustains the Universe; for them it is too painful to contemplate life without God. Nietzsche's famous parable of the madman is a landmark in modern intellectual history and deserves to be savored in full:

> Have you not heard of that madman who lit a lantern in the bright morning hours, ran to the market place, and cried incessantly, "I seek God! I seek God!"

As many of those who did not believe in God were standing around just then, he provoked much laughter. "Why, did he get lost?" said one. "Did he lose his way like a child?" said another. "Or is he hiding?" "Is he afraid of us?" "Has he gone on a voyage?" "Or emigrated?" Thus they yelled and laughed. The madman jumped into their midst and pierced them with his glances. "Whither is God?" he cried. "I shall tell you. We have killed him—you and I. All of us are his murderers. But how have we done this? How were we able to drink up the sea? Who gave us the sponge to wipe away the entire horizon? What did we do when we unchained this earth from the sun? Whither is it moving now? Whither are we moving now? Away from all suns? Are we not plunging continually? Backwards, sideward, forward, in all directions? Is there any up or down left? Are we not straying as through an infinite nothing? Do we not feel the breath of empty space? Has it not become colder? Is not night and more night coming on all the while? Must not lanterns be lit in the morning? Do we not hear anything yet of the noise of the gravediggers who are burying God? Do we not smell anything yet of God's decomposition? Gods too decompose. God is dead. God remains dead. And we have killed him. How shall we, the murderers of all murderers, comfort ourselves? What was holiest and most powerful of all that the world has yet owned has bled to death under our knives? Who will wipe this blood off us? What water is there for us to clean ourselves? What festivals of atonement, what sacred games shall we have to invent? Is not the greatness of this deed too great for us? Must not we ourselves become gods simply to seem worthy of it? There has never been a greater deed; and whoever will be born after us—for the sake of this deed he will be part of a higher history than all history hitherto." Here the madman fell silent and looked again at his listeners; and they too were silent and stared at him in astonishment. At last he threw his lantern on the ground, and it broke and went out. "I come too early," he said then; "my time has not come yet. This tremendous event is still on its way, still wandering—it has not yet reached the ears of man. Lightning and thunder require time, the light of the stars requires time, deeds require time even after they are done, before they can be seen or heard. This deed is still more distant from them than the most distant stars—and yet they have done it themselves." It has been related further that on this same day the madman entered divers churches and there sang his requiem aeternam deo. Led out and called to account, he is said to have replied each time, "What are these churches now if they are not the tombs and sepulchers of God?"[3]

Nietzsche scholars have long debated what exactly he meant by his announcement that "God is dead. God remains dead. And we have killed him." The philosopher Martin Heidegger famously asked, "Which God is dead?" and then went on to say that Nietzsche's dead God was the "morality God" (the Judge and Heavenly Paymaster) who was not worthy of belief in the first place. Nietzsche meant that we must kill a certain conception or interpretation of God. For Heidegger, Nietzsche was "that passionate seeker after God," a reference to the fact that his latter-day Diogenes comes into the marketplace announcing "I seek God, I seek God." Indeed, the philosopher Julian Young argues in *Nietzsche's Philosophy of Art* that "Nietzsche's intellectual quest can be characterized as 'proving that God, after all, exists.'" [4]

Some have seized on the parable's final question ("*What are these churches now if they are not the tombs and sepulchers of God?*") to argue that Nietzsche's attack was against false religion as practiced by many believers rather than against the notion of Deity *per se*. It is a familiar cry today, one that emanates not only from despairing or lapsed Christians, but from those of all religions when challenged by modern secularism or deadly acts of terrorism. For example, a Muslim bridegroom—confronted by the death of his father and father-in-law at the bombing of his own wedding on November 9, 2005 at a hotel in Amman, Jordan—faced the international media and insisted, "This is *not* Islam." That is, those who claim to be followers of a religion do not always act in ways that accurately reflect the God in whom they purport to believe.

Others have argued that there is a major inconsistency in Nietzsche's fable, for is it not absurd to think that humans can kill God? According to the classical/medieval scholastic definition of God, one of God's attributes is "aseity" (Latin *a se esse* "being from oneself"*)* which is usually translated "self-existence." God is not dependent for her existence on any other reality apart from herself. In abstract theological terminology God has absolute ontological independence—that is, exists without reference to anyone/anything else. God just *is*, without beginning or end. How could such an existence be terminated except by some reality capable of destroying God? But there can be no such reality, because God came into being without the involvement of any other agency and is eternal. Humanity is not capable of murdering God because God is not a being (like ourselves). Rather, as Paul Tillich expressed it, "God is Being-itself." God cannot be said to exist in the same way that we humans exist.

These are ingenious attempts at making Nietzsche a Christian believer, but the bulk of scholarship admits that Nietzsche had peered over the precipice into the abyss of nihilism and, instead of shrinking back in terror, plunged headlong into it. Once there, Nietzsche apparently replaced belief in God with the myth of the eternal return/recurrence. But that is another story . . .

In this book you have been introduced to four possible ways of responding to Nietzsche's madman. The first way, described as "panentheism," is best illustrated in the books of Bishop John Shelby Spong.[5] It is what might also be described as "liberal Christianity." The second way, often labeled "non-realism," is reflected in the writings of Don Cupitt and Lloyd Geering. It is "radical Christianity." The third way is the populist "grassroots" spirituality revolution of the new millennium that disturbs and challenges both liberalism and fundamentalism. The fourth way is to be a religious naturalist, investing nature with divinity and recycling God as an ecological imperative.

How, then, would each of these—radical Christians, liberal Christians, those in the spirituality revolution, and religious naturalists—respond to Nietzsche's madman?

Radicals like Cupitt and Geering would embrace the madman and follow him dancing around the town, echoing his proclamation, "We have killed him, you and I." For them, God is a human creation: the supernatural content of the God-idea no longer works and so it is time to reinvest it with new meaning for a new age. All religious doctrines must be understood ethically and existentially—they are guiding myths to live by as we strive to create a new heaven here on earth, and our sword and buckler against the specter of nihilism. Cupitt and Geering would try to cheer up the madman by insisting that he had *not* come "too early" for people. In fact, our watchword should be a currently popular saying: *carpe diem*—seize the day, seize the moment—because all we have is *this* life, and true religion is an affirmation of this life. We must say "Yes to life" in full acknowledgment of its contingency and transitoriness.

Geering and Cupitt would be joined by the religious naturalists in pointing Nietzsche in another direction—the protection and care of the planet. We must work towards establishing "tomorrow's god," providing a just, peaceful and equitable world for all, both human and creature alike. The love of God must be replaced by a new-found reverence for our global home, and the task of religious people is to hand on to following generations an integrated ecosystem in the best possible condition.

The liberal Bishop Spong would look at the madman and reply, "I agree with your non-theism; to be sure, the traditional God in whom the Church has so heavily invested to prop up an ailing institution is dead. Indeed, the God of supernatural theism is no longer persuasive. But that is not the whole story." He would then insist on the existence of what William James affirmed in *The Varieties of Religious Experience* as 'a 'More'—a something greater, an extra dimension of reality beyond our wildest imaginings that calls to everyone from the depths of their own being.[6] He would continue: "A God-presence invades me, whom I call Love. God is the one in whom the cosmos is, yet God is more than the cosmos. Beyond all the names that the different religions use to label their divinities remains a Mystery." And he might close by saying, "Come, let me take you to a psychiatrist, and after he helps you recognize the source and nature of your semi-delusional perceptions, we shall discuss your ideas further."

Those in the grassroots spirituality revolution would be part of the crowd, but instead of laughing at the madman they would advise him that what he was really seeking was a new spirituality. They would hand him a brochure to join them at the local "Mind, Body, Spirit" Festival where he would have an abundance of opportunities to find the "inner" God. His anger would then be assuaged with an assortment of spiritual therapies, his mind cleansed, his body healed, and his inner self transformed. Having chosen one or several from among the many paths to enlightenment, he would discover holistic healing and his troubled soul would be stilled.

These, then, are the responses to "the God problem." But which way should one go? In this concluding chapter I will point out some of the problems associated with each of the responses, and finally I will show that taking any of these routes will necessarily change the very nature of Christianity.

## NON-REALISM

First, then, is non-realism a credible position to hold, and what happens to Christianity if it is widely adopted?

Perhaps the most vociferous opponent of non-realism has been the atheist Michael Goulder, whose own unease with believing in God led him in 1981 to resign as an Episcopalian minister. Goulder neatly sets out the difficulties that face a non-realist Christian:

> I certainly do not think such a position absurd or dishonest; but I think it paradoxical, and such paradoxes are only for the very clever. Religious stories are valued because they are thought to be in some sense true; liturgies are carried through because they are thought to put us in some relationship with a real world beyond; if religious language is used to back ethical prescriptions, it is because it is still felt to reflect metaphysical belief. The magic is gone from the Christmas stocking when the identity of Santa Claus is known; we may carry the ritual on for a few years for the nostalgia, but its days are numbered. Beliefs are not a dispensable superstructure, as a ship may sail on without its topmast. . . . Non-academic people—and that includes non-academic churchmen and saints—would feel that there is something bogus about saying prayers to a non-existent God, thanking him for an atonement he has not made, by the death of one who is not his Son; and that if the metaphysics are false and the Christian story is a myth . . . then no emotional response can spring naturally from it, and no ethic can be grounded in it. . . . If belief in God is not a valid option, then neither is Christianity a valid option.[7]

Interestingly, Goulder's criticism of non-realism echoes Nietzsche's complaint in *The Twilight of the Idols* that Christianity is a complete system, and if you get rid of belief in an objective God the whole edifice will collapse.[8] It also finds support in a modern-day theologian like Marcus Borg who affirms that "at the heart of Christianity is God (and) without a robust affirmation of the reality of God, Christianity makes no sense."[9] For Goulder, non-realism is atheism in disguise. Unwilling to adopt Cupitt's position—he considers it to be "academic double-talk"—he decided that the only honest course of action was to leave organized religion, since the churches are "locked for ever in the ice-floes of theological contradiction."[10]

Similarly, but on the other side of the theological divide, the feminist theologian Daphne Hampson represents those who are mystified why anyone would want to affirm both the continuity of Christianity and the discontinuity of its essential underpinning—a realist understanding of God. Hampson, labelling herself a "non-Christian realist," is convinced of the continuing validity of the term "God" in referring to an objective reality that is not simply "an idealized notion of human beings." Yet because of her feminist critique of Christianity, she must separate herself from the Christian tradition. Finding it irredeemably sexist, she leaves the Church, having found other strategies for survival. A similar case is that of Mary Daly, who argues that the women's movement is an "exodus" community in which people can express their belief in transcendence without being constrained by the irredeemably patriarchal Christian tradition. In a dramatic manifesto delivered to the congregation at the Harvard Memorial Chapel in 1971, she insisted that the only possible route is "to affirm our faith in ourselves and our will to transcendence by rising and walking out together."[11]

It would seem that non-realism raises the difficult question of whether the Christian message can survive without what academic theologians call an ontological referent. In short, can one have Christianity without God? Would permitting Christians to be card-carrying non-realists mark the end of the faith as it has been traditionally taught? For Marcus Borg it is much more than a scholarly quibble:

> Is God real? This is the central religious question in modern Western culture.[12]

Clearly, Cupitt and Geering see much more to Christianity than belief in an objective God. It has a story or myth that is retold or re-enacted daily and weekly in ritual; it has an ethical system and it's a powerful cultural dimension. And since for many the word "God" has lost its supernatural referent and thus its credibility, we can dispense with metaphysics and reinterpret the myth to suit our postmodern worldview. The symbol "God" can be reinterpreted to represent the highest and best of human ideals. That our religions have human origins suggests that they still fulfil a human need; and having created them, we can reinvent them. Don Cupitt sums up the situation persuasively:

> Religion is primarily not about supernatural belief, but about hope. It is our communal way of generating dreams of how we and our life and our world might be made better. We prepare ourselves for the dream, and we start to think about how we might actually start to make it all come true. My suggestion . . . has been that the so-called "decline of religion" is people's abandonment en masse of the kind of ecclesiastical religion that promised comfort and

reassurance in the face of death. Instead, we should see religious thought and practice as imaginative and utopian. Religion is a communal way of reimagining and remaking the self and the world. It is what we are to live *by* and what we are to live *for*. At a time when political thought is very unadventurous, and when the world is becoming overwhelmingly dominated by technology, we need religion as much as ever. We need it as a human, value-creating *activity*.[13]

### PANENTHEISM

The second option—that of clinging to the objectivity of God—is championed by Bishop Spong. He agrees with Cupitt that "God" is a human word, but insists that it points to a reality that human words can never exhaust. The word is a human construct; the reality to which it points is not.

But does it still make sense to cling to that sliver of objectivity? Can one find valid reasons to cling to an ineffable deity, or is it all a sort of desperate rearguard action? Has not the scientific worldview dispensed with such a notion long ago? In religion, as in many other areas of life, we can recognize an ancient and well-established culture of dependency. Many people seem to require that "something out-there" to lean on, however minimally. Why must Spong fiercely guard that tiny speck of objectivity, that feeling that there is, there must be, something Real out there to which all the symbolism refers—even though he cannot define or even describe it? As Sam Harris points out, this can lead to all sorts of irrational beliefs:

> It is perfectly absurd for religious moderates to suggest that a rational human being can believe in God simply because this belief makes him happy, relieves his fear of death or gives his life meaning. The absurdity becomes obvious the moment we swap the notion of God for some other consoling proposition: Imagine, for instance, that a man wants to believe that there is a diamond buried somewhere in his yard that is the size of a refrigerator. No doubt it would feel uncommonly good to believe this. Just imagine what would happen if he then followed the example of religious moderates and maintained this belief along pragmatic lines: When asked why he thinks that there is a diamond in his yard that is thousands of times larger than any yet discovered, he says things like, "This belief gives my life meaning," or "My family and I enjoy digging for it on Sundays," or "I wouldn't want to live in a universe where there wasn't a diamond buried in my backyard that is the size of a refrigerator." Clearly these responses are inadequate. But they are worse than that. They are the responses of a madman or an idiot.[14]

Spong's proposed reformation of Christianity entails further difficulties. He agrees that religious people experience God in different ways through the particular lens of the religion to which they belong, but this raises the question of the value and truth of every purported experience of God. Is the religious experience of the Christian, Hindu, Muslim, Sikh or Buddhist an incomplete apprehension of a greater reality called God? A popular analogy based on an ancient Buddhist parable of the blind men and the elephant is often invoked to show that all religions are valid ways to describe God. The story tells of four blind men who discover an elephant. Never having encountered such a thing before, they grope about, seeking to understand and describe this new phenomenon. One grasps the trunk and concludes it is a snake. Another explores one of the elephant's legs and describes it as a tree. A third finds the elephant's tail and announces that it is a rope. The fourth blind man, after examining the elephant's side, concludes that it is a wall. Each in his blindness describes one aspect of the same thing: an elephant. Yet each perceives that thing in a radically different way.[15] Professors of comparative religion especially love this story, because it makes all religions equally "true" in their description of God. And many theologians see in it an analogy to the different religions of the world—they are describing the same thing in radically different ways. From this, they assert, one should conclude that no individual religion has a corner on truth, but that all should be viewed as having essential and equal validity.

Of course, powerful evidence can be adduced to support the opposite proposal—that our several religions are intrinsically incompatible with one another. Either Jesus rose from the dead and will be returning to earth to "judge the living and the dead" or he will not. Either the Koran is the infallible word of God or it isn't. It would seem that most religions make explicit claims about the fact that people should follow its beliefs *and no other*. Besides, as I showed in chapter 1, the sheer profusion of these incompatible claims is what has created an enduring basis for conflict. How, then, can it be argued that all paths lead to the same God or the 'More'? Will Muslim, Hindu, Sikh, and Christian believers accept the validity of each other's experience of the sacred? Indeed, every religion has suffered from disputes amongst believers who allegedly worship the same God: Protestant versus Catholic, Sunni versus Shiite, etc. Christian theologians have responded to the existence of differing religions by adopting one of the following three paradigms. The pluralist paradigm accepts that other religions are equally salvific paths to the one God and that Christianity's claim to be the only path must be rejected. The exclusivist paradigm asserts that other religions testify to humankind's inherent sinfulness and are thus erroneous, while Christianity offers the only valid path to salvation. The inclusivist paradigm affirms the salvific presence of God in non-Christian religions while still maintaining that Christ is the definitive and authoritative revelation of God.[16] The recent case of Bishop Carlton Pearson, whose Higher Dimensions Family Church in Oklahoma has been forced into foreclosure because of his adoption of the pluralist paradigm, highlights the dangers of being a Christian minister who accepts the validity of other religions. A former evangelical superstar who was courted by the Bush administration, he is now ostracized by his fellow Christians.[17] It would seem that religious pluralism raises as many questions as answers.

Moreover, what does it mean to say that one has experienced the God-presence? Its very subjectivity calls into question the objectivity of which it claims to speak. How dependable is religious experience? Rather than rehearse here all the arguments against religious experience, I shall only note that the phenomenon, in its many varieties, is not necessarily as trustworthy as its advocates suppose. One telling piece of testimony by Michael Goulder should suffice to make the point:

> I have frequently taught classes of clergy in recent years in which the topic of (religious) experience has come up and I have often been impressed with the honest way in which some of the finest clergy have admitted to never having had a religious experience. I remember a Catholic priest saying, "No, I've never had what I would call an experience of God"; and a Lutheran pastor said to me, "Other people talk about experiences, but it does not generally boil down to much". . . . Religious experience is, it seems to me, quite a rare feature of life for clergy and laity alike. Some have never had it; few claim to have it often. . . . It is very rare to hear a sermon on prayer that sounds convincing—or indeed to read an article on or a book about God at all that carries conviction. It is all these cases of the *absence* (of God) which must strike a chill in the heart of the driven-snow Christian.[18]

Spong assumes that "religious experience is either a perception of a reality beyond the boundaries of our typical limits or a delusion created as a coping device by those who cannot tolerate, as that which is ultimate, a vision of meaninglessness."[19] Apparently he cannot envisage a non-realist interpretation of religious experience. But for Cupitt a spiritual intuition or response in no way presupposes supernatural content. Religious bliss is attained not by contacting something or someone outside us but by acknowledging the cosmos to be outsideless. In contrast to the Christian concept of religious ecstasy (literally: to be "out of oneself") in which the believer is caught up in finding Someone (God) outside the known world, Cupitt coined the term "entostasy," which means to "jump back into ourselves" and accept the world as it is. This does not mean being a fatalist, but simply acknowledging and accepting the fact that we are alone. There is no God, and the responsibility for all that happens is ours. As the non-realist prayer expresses it: "God has no hands but our hands, no feet, but our feet. . . ." We are accountable for the future of the Universe, our own lives and the lives of those around us. In short, there is "a purely immanent, *for me*, living, moving unity of everything."

> We give up everything and suddenly find eternal happiness, on the surface only and just Now, where Be-ing pours quietly forth into the dance of meanings and the flickering play of the most transient phenomena. That's bliss; it is "the

*Theol. present throughout the universe; said of God; distinguished from Transcendent.*

*Cupitt, 1998*

mysticism of secondariness," and it is what I am here calling the Revelation of Being—joyous acceptance of the way everything *turns out,* or just *happens to be.* It is high-speed ravishment, like lightning: it is sudden glory. It is what Carlyle calls "natural supernaturalism." It is eternal happiness, briefly, in and *with* the here and now.[20]

\# According to Cupitt, religious experience is the rapturous attention to the passing moment that occurs when we recognize that this life is all there is and we must love it now before it ceases to be. It is, as Richard Holloway explains, no different from what poets and artists have been advocating over the centuries: "All art is trying to get us to pay attention, to look at life and love it before we go from the fire-lit banqueting hall out into the winter's darkness."[21]

## THE SPIRITUALITY REVOLUTION

The third option is the spirituality revolution. What should we make of this smorgasbord of therapeutic modalities and programmes? Cupitt, for example, professes himself unsure about the vast array of spiritualities that have entered the religious supermarket, observing that they have created formless anarchy and often commit the same error as traditional religions by producing dogmatic teachings dispensed by gurus and shamans.

> The greatest and commonest mistake in religious thought is that made by the millions of people who today embrace 'spirituality' and New Age thinking without first clearing their heads. They rush uncritically into a tiny jumble of ideas: they have not sufficiently purged themselves of Platonism and so forth, and therefore, instead of escaping from the horrors of the past, they merely repeat them. We need to train ourselves to be thoroughly sceptical and emptied out before we can learn to think more clearly.[22]

On the surface, this seems to be a reasonable assessment. If the madman had followed the advice of the grassroots and gone along to "The Mind, Body, Spirit" Festival in any capital city in the Western world he might have experienced a whole host of outlandish and esoteric offerings that stretch the limits of credulity and rationality, as this account from Sydney, Australia, reveals:

> I've paid my $13 admission fee. I've grabbed my show bag (courtesy of Nature Care College) and now join me on a stroll around these seminars and meet some of the festival's more colourful characters. There's Madi Nolan, whose impressive credentials include the fact that she cured wandering spirits in an Indian burial ground and brought new life to failed businesses. She offers Black Hat Feng Shui cures for her clients who will develop the skills to 'capture the images of earth ley lines, vortex centers and nature spirits.' Part of the secret of her success is that she has a powerful magic altar cloth from a monastery in Nepal. . . . Or if your love life has been a bit flat lately, you can learn from Oceana and Icarus . . . you can get tips on Tantric lovemaking and relation-

ships and learn how to reconcile your sexuality and spirituality. They promote themselves as the world's foremost Tantra teaching married couple who met at sunrise at the top of a mountain in the Himalayas. . . . It's hard to resist an expert on the human soul, its origin in the universe, and its history on this planet. That's Ruthe Rendely, who has channelled angelic energies since 1995 when a high angel approached her to bring out the Seraphim Blueprint, an angelic system that was developed for the benefit of humanity in Atlantean times. Ruthe will also tell me how I can establish an abiding connection with one of the highest angels in the universe, the archangel Michael. . . . Then there's the workshop of Kerrie Edwards-Ticehurst where, using creative visualizations, meditation, chakras, clairvoyancy and clairaudience, you can learn to speed up your vibrations, so making it easier to make contact with the other side. Then through palm reading, jewellery reading, and interpretation of your aura you can 'travel to your temple to meet your guides and then journey into past lives with these friends'.[23]

Clearly, this writer was unimpressed with some of the more bizarre offerings at the Festival; but can *all* spiritualities be characterized as hogwash, collections of "weirdos," and a resurgence of the 1960s hippy revolution? Can one distinguish between the false shaman and the genuine spirit person—and if so, how determine what kinds of belief are acceptable today? If our criterion is that they must be reasonable, most recognized religions would likewise fail the test. What is more irrational: a Christian believing in the bodily resurrection, or a devotee of pranic healing believing in the ability of the body to heal itself by a process of energy therapy? What is more absurd: the conviction that Satan is literally at work persuading people to commit evil, or that the practice of feng shui can affect your physical and spiritual well being? What is more unreasonable: the belief that legalising gay marriage will incur God's wrath and bring disaster upon a nation, or that we may get in touch with the spirits of our former selves in another lifetime? Perhaps *caveat emptor* is a warning that applies to all religions and spiritualities! The buyer—and all forms of religion/spirituality cost something—must be extremely cautious of the intentions of those peddling religious wares; and should scrutinize their claims and beliefs very carefully. Moreover, many of these new spirituality tools and practitioners are becoming sufficiently mainstream to be frequently used in the corporate and religious worlds. Take for example neuro-linguistic programming, walking the labyrinth (made popular by Lauren Artress at Grace Cathedral, San Francisco), the Enneagram, Thomas Moore and the care of the soul, holistic healing techniques, and ecological concerns. What was weird twenty years ago seems normal today.

Moreover, the rise of the spirituality revolution poses important questions for Christianity. If in postmodernity the various notions of the gods have become disseminated by language within and even across cultures, then why should we limit ourselves to remything Christianity? What is so special about the Jesus story that it warrants such attention? Does Christianity offer something unique to people in search for meaning? Why should these people be interested in Jesus if, as it seems, their religious creativity is already discovering inspiration in a myriad of sources, both ancient and modern? If Christianity opts for non-realism, will it strike a chord with many people's spiritual search? Although they may dismiss notions like deity and sainthood, even today people still seek something beyond themselves to venerate and be guided by.

### RELIGIOUS NATURALISM

The fourth option, religious naturalism, changes Christianity by refocusing its attention from an objective spiritual being to the earth's ecosystem. Rather than worship a deity from another plane of existence, we may well stand in awe of the self-evolving universe:

> To believe in God is to commit oneself to a particular way of ordering one's life and action. It is to devote oneself to working towards a fully humane world within the ecological restraints here on planet Earth, while standing in piety and awe before the profound mysteries of existence.[24]

For proponents of this programme, Christianity in the twenty-first century takes on a green glow. Its rites and festivals are transformed from reverence for a divine being to the acknowledgment of the sacredness of nature.[25] It rejects the kind of religious fundamentalism that ignores the plight of the earth in the belief that the final Battle of Armageddon predicts the degradation of the cosmos and foretells the establishment of God's reign on earth. The divinely imposed Ten Commandments are replaced by a voluntary human protocol of Ten Resolutions:

1. Let us take time to stand in awe of this self-evolving universe.
2. Let us marvel at the living ecosphere of this planet.
3. Let us set a supreme value on all forms of life.
4. Let us develop a lifestyle that preserves the balance of the planetary ecosystem.
5. Let us refrain from all activities that endanger the future of any species.
6. Let us devote ourselves to maximizing the future of all living creatures.
7. Let us set the needs of the coming global society before those of ourselves, our tribe, society, or nation.
8. Let us learn to value the human relationships that bind us together into social groups.
9. Let us learn to appreciate the total cultural legacy we have received from the past.

10. Let us accept in a self-sacrificing fashion the responsibility now laid upon us all for the future of our species and of all planetary life.[26]

The "greening" of Christianity thus outlined stands in marked contrast, and indeed direct contradiction, to much of the historic teaching of the churches. Instead of being lords of the universe and the pinnacle of creation, we must view ourselves as part of an interconnected web of existence. The responsibility for the future of the planet rests with us. We cannot look to another world and another life beyond this one, but must commit ourselves to an ecological imperative that will benefit succeeding generations.

### CONCLUSION

In summing up, let me first reiterate the intention of this book: to outline what I perceive to be the most crucial area of religious discourse for the New Millennium—what I have called the "God problem." Reduced to its simplest terms, the issue is whether to adopt a realist or a non-realist understanding of God. Is God real or simply a symbol of our ultimate concern? Can the perception of an objective God be replaced by a concern for the preservation and continuation of the cosmos? Can nature become the locus of the sacred?

In this book I have used the writings of Don Cupitt and Lloyd Geering as templates for non-realism, and Bishop Spong and the spirituality revolution as templates for realism. You will have noted that I incline toward non-realism; the reason is that I find it the most *intellectually* compelling reading of Christianity. I am nonetheless poignantly aware that we, myself included, whose cultural roots are in Western Christianity find it *emotionally* difficult to throw off the final vestige of belief in a being, essence, or principle greater than ourselves. Perhaps it is true, as Nietzsche remarked as long ago as 1882, that while our ancient belief in God will haunt the human race for thousands of years, it is our perennial task to "vanquish" this antique superstition.[27] Indeed, I think it probable that the somewhat ambiguous position expressed by Richard Holloway is where most of us find ourselves:

> As far as the status of God is concerned, I find that the needle on my own dial trembles midway between non-realism (God is a human invention) and critical realism (there is a mystery out there, but we are inextricably involved in its interpretation and never get it with complete purity). On the one hand I cannot return to an understanding of religious claims that is pre-critical; on the other hand, I am not quite prepared to reduce the whole of religious experience to human projection, though much of it clearly is.[28]

That in a nutshell has been the central theme of this book: the problem of God!

Which religious or spiritual pathway will *you* choose to walk?

# NOTES

## INTRODUCTION

1  Funk, *Honest to Jesus.*

2  See especially Funk, *A Credible Jesus.*

3  This is shown clearly in the titles of books, *The Once and Future Jesus* and *The Once and Future Faith*. Moreover, the addition of new Fellows who were not specialist Biblical scholars (for example, Karen Armstrong, Don Cupitt and Lloyd Geering) reveals the interest that was generated in the Second Agenda. For a detailed examination of those churches who have embraced new ways of understanding the Christian gospel see Taussig, *A New Spiritual Home.*

4  Funk, "A Faith for the Future" in *The Once and Future Faith*, 8–9.

5  Donovan, *Christianity Rediscovered*, 56–57.

6  Hoover, "Incredible Creed, Credible Faith" in *The Once and Future Faith,* 81.

7  Harris, "An Atheist Manifesto."

8  Funk, "A Faith for the Future" in *The Once and Future Faith*, 15–16.

9  Goodenough, "There are two flavors of God people."

## CHAPTER ONE
## Setting the Scene: The Terror of God

1  Ruthven, *Fundamentalism*, 4.

2  Nietzsche, *The Twilight of the Idols* and *The Anti-Christ*; Flew, *God and Philosophy*; Russell, *Why I Am Not a Christian*; Barth, *Church Dogmatics*; Lewis, *Mere Christianity*; Swinburne, *The Existence of God.*

3  This is obviously not a comprehensive list of Christian ministers who have been accused of heresy. "The mental inquisition" is a title of a book by Paul Collins (Overlook Press, 2002) with interviews of those, including himself, who had been under investigation by the Roman Catholic Congregation for the Doctrine of the Faith. Collins resigned from the priesthood in 2001.

4  Harris, "An Atheist Manifesto." *Licensed Insanities* is a title of a book by John Bowker.

5  Ruthven, *Fundamentalism*, 182.

6  McCourt, *Angela's Ashes*, 124 (my bold).

7  Armstrong, *Battle for God.*

8  Salman Rushdie was condemned to death by the former Iranian spiritual leader Ayatollah Khomeini on February 14, 1989, after publishing *Satanic Verses*. He spent many years in hiding being protected by British security police. In 1993 Rushdie's Norwegian publisher William Nygaard was wounded in an attack outside his house. However, in September 1998 the Iranian government announced that the state was not going to put into effect the *fatwa* or encourage anybody to do so. Despite that action, in February 1999 Ayatollah Hassan Sanei promised a $2.8 million reward for

killing the author. Rushdie is now living openly in the United States. Homosexuals are constantly condemned by both Christian and Islamic fundamentalists. Indeed, for some Christian groups the attack on the United States on 9/11 was sent by God as a judgment for permitting homosexuals to be part of American society. It is estimated that since 1979 the Islamic Republic of Iran has executed four thousand lesbians and gays for "the crime of homosexuality." For a good discussion on how Christians have used the Bible to justify hatred of homosexuals see Spong, *The Sins of Scripture*, 111–42.

9   Harris, *The End of Faith*, 25.

10   Howard, *Basil Hume*.

11   Huntingdon, *The Clash of Civilizations*.

12   President George W. Bush was reported to have told the Palestinian foreign minister, Nabil Shaath, that God directed him to "fight these terrorists in Afghanistan" and "end the tyranny in Iraq" (*The Guardian*, October 7, 2005). President Mahmoud Ahmadinejad's speech to the United Nations General Assembly in September, 2005, was littered with apocalyptic references, ending with a messianic appeal to God to "hasten the emergence of your last repository, the Promised One."

13   Sting's song "Russians" is from the Album *The Dream of Blue Turtles*. The full text is:

> In Europe and America, there's a growing feeling of hysteria
>
> Conditioned to respond to all the threats
>
> In the rhetorical speeches of the Soviets
>
> Mr. Krushchev said we will bury you
>
> I don't subscribe to this point of view
>
> It would be such an ignorant thing to do
>
> If the Russians love their children too
>
> How can I save my little boy from Oppenheimer's deadly toy
>
> There is no monopoly of common sense
>
> On either side of the political fence
>
> We share the same biology
>
> Regardless of ideology
>
> Believe me when I say to you
>
> I hope the Russians love their children too
>
> There is no historical precedent
>
> To put words in the mouth of the president
>
> There's no such thing as a winnable war
>
> It's a lie we don't believe anymore
>
> Mr. Reagan says we will protect you
>
> I don't subscribe to this point of view
>
> Believe me when I say to you
>
> I hope the Russians love their children too

We share the same biology

Regardless of ideology

What might save us me and you

Is that the Russians love their children too

14  Harris makes this same point: "The men who committed the atrocities of September 11 were certainly not "cowards," as they were repeatedly described in the Western media, nor were they lunatics in any ordinary sense. They were men of faith—perfect faith, as it turns out—and this, it must finally be acknowledged, is a terrible thing to be" (*End of Faith*, 67). This has not been fully understood by Westerners, many of whom do not believe in an after-life, or by those who believe it is a reward for 'doing good'. Harris correctly concludes: "There is little possibility of having a *cold* war with an Islamist regime armed with long-range nuclear weapons. A cold war requires that the parties be mutually deterred by the threat of death." (*End of Faith*, 128). Indeed, the estimated one million deaths in the Iran-Iraq War (1980–88) is testament to the deep seated belief in martyrdom by both Sunni and Shiite Muslims. One wonders what the consequences would have been if one side had had nuclear capability in the 1980s.

15  The Madrid train bombings on March 11, 2004 were not conducted by suicide bombers. The Muslim terrorists placed the bombs on the train in backpacks and then left the trains before they exploded. However, a few weeks later when they were cornered by security forces in their apartments they committed suicide using explosives strapped to their bodies.

16  Geering, *Fundamentalism*, 44.

17  Harris, *End of Faith*, 224–25.

18  Another piece of wisdom from Sting from his song, "History will teach us nothing," Album, *Nothing Like the Sun*, A and M records, Los Angeles, 1987.

19  The working title of the book is: "The Escaped Prisoner: when God is a monster."

20  Transcript from MEMRITV: available at http://memritv.org. See also, John M. Broder, "For Muslim who says violence destroys Islam, violent threats," *New York Times*, March 11, 2006. I thank Elizabeth J. Kenyon of EJK Technical Publishing Services for her help with this section on radical women in Islam.

21  Taken from Taslima Nasrin's website at http://taslimanasrin.com/index2.html

22  I will use Cupitt and Geering to show that Harris is wrong to assert that all Christians believe in God (Harris, *End of Faith*, 246, endnote 30).

23  Irshad Manji, "When denial can kill; why we Muslims must admit that our religion might be motivating the bombers," *Time*, July 17, 2005.

24  Ruthven, *Fundamentalism*, 34.

25  Cupitt, *The Sea of Faith*, 185.

26  Fortunately, many groups are challenging the fundamentalist take-over of religion; see the list of liberal religious associations in Appendix 1.

27  Richard Dawkins, *The Guardian*, December 28, 2004.

28  Goodenough, "The Religious Dimensions of the Biological Narrative," 604.

29  See the book of the same name by Malise Ruthven.

30 The Very Reverend Philip Jensen's commencement sermon of March 2003 when he was installed as the Anglican Dean of Sydney, as quoted in McGillion, *The Chosen Ones*, 197 (my bold).

## CHAPTER TWO

## Panentheism: John Shelby Spong

1 Spong, *Why Christianity Must Change or Die*, 4.

2 Slogan on Center for Progressive Christian spirituality webpage: http://www.progressivespirituality.net.

3 This subject will be dealt with in detail in chapter 4.

4 Significantly, Marcus Borg whose endorsement of panentheism is the same as that of Spong refuses to use the phrase "end of theism." For Borg, it is a confusing term that "to many people, this sounds like rejection of the very idea of God; in their minds, not surprisingly, the alternative to theism is atheism" (*The Heart of Christianity*, 69).

5 Spong, *Here I Stand*, 468.

6 Spong, *A New Christianity for a New World*, 240.

7 Spong, *A New Christianity for a New World*, x.

8 For example Stacey, *Who Cares?*

9 Bowden (ed.), *Thirty Years of Honesty*, 73 (my bold).

10 Spong, quoting Funk, *A New Christianity for a New World*, 228–29.

11 Spong, *Here I Stand*, 70.

12 Spong, *A New Christianity for a New World*, 131.

13 Spong, *A New Christianity for a New World*, 182.

14 Spong, *Why Christianity Must Change or Die*, 147

15 Spong, "The theistic God is dead," in Steven Waldman (ed.), *From the Ashes*, 54–60.

16 Spong, *A New Christianity for a New World*, 200.

17 Channel 7 interview, Australia, 2003.

18 Spong, *The Sins of Scripture*, 25.

19 Spong, *A New Christianity for a New World*, 216.

20 As set out by Jenks, *Faithfutures Guide No. 2*, 37 (my addition in italics).

21 Spong, *A New Christianity for a New World*, 245.

## CHAPTER THREE

## Non-realism: Don Cupitt and Lloyd Geering

1 Transcript of BBC TV series, *The Sea of Faith*, 1984.

2 Freeman, *God in Us*, 28.

3 Cupitt, *Taking Leave of God*, xii.

4 See my *Odyssey on the Sea of Faith* and *Surfing on the Sea of Faith*.

5 Edwards, *Tradition and Truth*, 96.

6 *Tradition and Truth*, 286.

7 Paterson, "Why I resigned."

8 Cupitt, *Radicals and the Future of the Church*, 16.

9 *Radicals and the Future of the Church*, 29.

10 *Radicals and the Future of the Church*, 5.

11 *Radicals and the Future of the Church*, 97.

12 *Radicals and the Future of the Church*, 122.

13 Cupitt, *Reforming Christianity*, 128.

14 *Reforming Christianity*, 136.

15 The Cupitt books which best illustrate these themes are indicated.

16 Cupitt, *Philosophy's Own Religion*, viii–ix.

17 Cupitt, *Reforming Christianity*, 123.

18 Geering, *Tomorrow's God*, 86.

19 *Tomorrow's God*, 194.

20 For his "Scenarios of the Future" see Geering, *The World to Come*, 135–149. The final chapter of the book is entitled: "A Faith for the Future."

21 Goodenough, *The Sacred Depths of Nature*, xv.

22 Geering, *Christianity without God*, 130, 119.

CHAPTER FOUR

### The Spirituality Revolution: Grassroots Spirituality

1 The main opponent of the secularization theory in the 1960s was David Martin of the London School of Economics.

2 Berger, *The Desecularization of the World*, 2.

3 Froma Harrop, *Providence* Journal, October 9, 2005.

4 In the United Kingdom research concerning the various religious experiences of its citizens has been conducted by The Religious Experience Research Centre. This was founded by the marine biologist Professor Sir Alister Hardy in 1969 as The Religious Experience Research Unit. He and his co-researchers gathered accounts of the religious experiences of ordinary folk and published them in a series of booklets. The Centre was originally situated in Oxford: from 1969–1989 at Manchester College and from 1989–1999 at Westminster College. Since 1999 it has been located at the University of Wales, Lampeter. For more information view http://www.lamp.ac.uk/trs/Main_pages/other_activities.htm.

• 5 Forman, *Grassroots Spirituality*, 4.

6 Tacey, *ReEnchantment*, 52.

7 Ballis and Bouma (eds.), *Religion in an Age of Change*, 8.

8 For more information see http://www.powerenergetics.com.

9 For more information see http://www.subud.org.

10 This forty percent is a national average. In some urban areas the figure might be as high as eighty percent.

11 Davie, "Europe: the exception that proves the rule" in Berger (ed.), *The Desecularization of the World*, 68. Her phrase 'believing without belonging' has been

used extensively by theologians to describe the British religious situation. Sutcliffe and Bowman make the apposite point that there is also an "under-explored corollary of 'belonging without believing'—through custom and social pressure," see Sutcliffe and Bowman (eds.), *Beyond New Age*, 3.

12 Midgley, "Spirited away."

13 "Spirited away."

14 Bruce, *God is Dead*, 44.

15 Bruce, "The New Age and Secularization" in Sutcliffe and Bowman (eds.), *Beyond New Age*, 233.

16 "The New Age and Secularization," 234.

17 Forman, *Grassroots Spirituality*, 51.

18 Heelas, "Sources of Significance beyond church and chapel" in Sutcliffe and Bowman (eds.), *Beyond New Age*, 243.

19 Carrette and King, *Selling Spirituality*, 172.

20 Pederby, *Third World Conundrum*, 91.

21 Midgley, "Spirited away."

22 Heelas in Sutcliffe and Bowman (eds.), *Beyond New Age*, 239.

23 Heelas and Woodhead, *The Spiritual Revolution*, 10.

24 Tacey, *ReEnchantment*, 262.

CHAPTER FIVE

Religious Naturalism: The Awe and Wonder of Nature

1 Cupitt, *The Revelation of Being*, 84–85. Cupitt mentions Hobbes, Berkeley and Hume as religious naturalists.

2 Collins, *God's Earth*, 122.

3 *God's Earth*, 247.

4 Spearritt, "Religion: It's Natural," 3.

5 Robbins, "When Christians Become Naturalists," 195–206.

6 Spearritt, "Religion: It's Natural," 3.

7 Dawkins, "Snake Oil and Holy Water," 1–2.

8 Cupitt, *Kingdom Come in Everyday Speech*, 88. The main difference between Rorty and Cupitt is that, for Cupitt, Christian metaphysical and symbolic language (if demythologized) can still inspire religious attitudes and feelings, whereas Rorty has no need of it.

9 Spearritt, "Religion: It's Natural," 4.

10 Goodenough, *The Sacred Depths of Nature*, 171.

11 Goodenough, "Religious Dimensions," 603. This is repeated in *The Sacred Depths of Nature*, 10 ("also" is omitted). The "credo of continuation" can also be found in "The Religious Dimensions of Biological Narrative," 612. Goodenough's other article is: "What Science Can and Cannot Offer to a Religious Narrative."

12 Gould, *Rocks of Ages*, 4.

13 *Rocks of Ages*, 9.

14  *Rocks of Ages*, 4.

15  Goodenough, "Religious Dimensions," 604.

16  "Religious Dimensions," 604.

17  Goodenough, *The Sacred Depths of Nature*, xvii.

18  Goodenough, "What Science Can Offer," 329.

19  Cf. chaps. 10 and 11 of Geering's, *The World to Come* with Goodenough's introduction to *The Sacred Depths of Nature*.

20  Goodenough, *The Sacred Depths of Nature*, 10.

21  *The Sacred Depths of Nature*, 12.

22  *The Sacred Depths of Nature*, 12–13.

23  *The Sacred Depths of Nature*, 149.

24  *The Sacred Depths of Nature*, 151.

25  *The Sacred Depths of Nature*, 151.

26  Cupitt, *The Revelation of Being*, 9.

27  *The Revelation of Being*, 8.

28  *The Revelation of Being*, 94.

29  Goodenough, *The Sacred Depths of Nature*, 169; Cupitt, *The Revelation of Being*, 10 (his italics).

30  Acknowledging a debt to her father, Edwin Goodenough (Professor of the History of Religion at Yale), she embraces her Methodist background by being an active member of Trinity Presbyterian Church, Washington (*The Sacred Depths of Nature*, ix–xi).

31  *The Sacred Depths of Nature*, 172–73.

32  Cupitt, *The Revelation of Being*, 94.

33  Webb, review of *The Sacred Depths of Nature*, 237.

34  Cupitt, *The Revelation of Being*, 94.

35  Malouf, *An Imaginary Life*, 7.

36  Charlesworth (ed.), *Religious Business*, xx.

37  Bentley and Hughes, *Australian Life and the Christian Faith*, 108.

38  Winton, *The Land's Edge*, 36–37.

39  Malouf, *A Spirit of Play*, 8.

40  For a good starting point see Victorin-Vangerud, "The Sacred Edge."

41  Geering, *The Greening of Christianity*, 32.

42  Thomas, *The Lives of a Cell*, 3.

43  Smuts, "Sanctifying the Cosmos."

CHAPTER SIX

## Conclusion

1  Funk, *The Once and Future Faith*, 17.

2  The traditional English translation of the title, *Die fröhliche Wissenschaft*, as *The Gay Science* is now obviously obsolete.

3  Nietzsche, *The Joyous Science*, section 125.

4  See Fraser, *Redeeming Nietzsche*, 1.

5  See also the works of Marcus Borg.

6  William James' *The Varieties of Religious Experience* was first published in 1902, so at the time would have been a challenging response to Nietzsche's *The Joyous Science*, written in 1882.

7  Goulder and Hick, *Why believe in God?*, 29–30.

8  Nietzsche, *Twilight of the Idols*, 80–81.

9  Borg, *The Heart of Christianity*, 61.

10  Goulder and Hick, *Why believe in God?*, 28.

11  Armstrong, *The Gospel According to Woman*, 302.

12  Borg, *The Heart of Christianity*, 61.

13  Cupitt, "Christianity after the Church," 11.

14  Harris, "An Atheist Manifesto."

15  The origins of the story are obscure but it seems that the story was first found in Pali Buddhist literature. The story was popularized by American poet John Godfrey Saxe (1816–1887) who expanded the four blind men to "six men of Hindostan."

16  For a good discussion of these viewpoints see D'Costa, *Theology and Religious Pluralism*.

17  See http://www.projo.com/religion/content/projo_20051224_rishun24.198077bf.html.

18  Goulder and Hick, *Why believe in God?*, 61–62. Interestingly, Marcus Borg asserts that "the experiential base of religion is very strong and ultimately its most persuasive ground." See Borg, *The Heart of Christianity*, 64. He thus agrees with both Spong and John Hick that religious experience is foundational for belief in God.

19  Spong, "A Christianity for tomorrow" in *The Once and Future Faith*, 69.

20  Cupitt, *The Revelation of Being*, 10.

21  Holloway, *Doubts and Loves*, 245.

22  Cupitt, *Emptiness and Brightness*, 23 (footnote).

23  Raiter, *Stirrings of the Soul*, 15–17.

24  Lloyd Geering quoting Gordon Kaufman, see Jones, *God, Galileo and Geering*, 163.

25  Geering, *The Greening of Christianity*, ch. 4.

26  *The Greening of Christianity*, 53–54.

27  Nietzsche, *Joyous Science*, 167.

28  Holloway, *Doubts and Loves*, 28–29.

# Appendix

| | |
|---|---|
| Westar Institute/Jesus Seminar | www.westarinstitute.org |
| The Jefferson Center | www.thejeffcenter.org |
| Sea of Faith (Australia) | www.sof-in-australia.org |
| Sea of Faith (New Zealand) | www.sof.wellington.net.nz |
| Sea of Faith (United Kingdom) | www.sofn.org.uk |
| Snowstar Institute | www.snowstarinstitute.org |
| Faith Futures Foundation | www.faithfutures.org |
| The Center for Progressive Christianity | www.tcpc.org |
| Arizona Foundation for Contemporary Theology | www.azfct.org |
| Christian Humanism | www.christianhumanism.org |
| The Secular Web | www.infidels.org |
| Whidbey Institute | www.whidbeyinsitute.org |
| Northwest Earth Institute | www.nwei.org |
| Institute on Religion in an Age of Science | www.iras.org |
| Americans United for Separation of Church and State | www.au.org |
| Humanistic Judaism | www.shj.org |
| Unitarian Universalist Association | www.uua.org |
| Liberal Islam Network | www.int.islamlib.com |
| Institute for the Secularization of Islamic Society | www.secularislam.org |
| Naturalism | www.naturalism.org |
| The Interfaith Alliance | wwww.interfaithalliance.org |

# Bibliography

Armstrong, Karen. *The Gospel According to Woman*. London: HarperCollins, 1986.

————. *The Battle for God: Fundamentalism in Judaism, Christianity and Islam*. London: HarperCollins, 2000.

Ballis, Peter H. and Gary D. Bouma eds. *Religion in an Age of Change*. Victoria: Christian Research Association, 1999.

Barth, Karl. *Church Dogmatics*. Edinburgh: T and T Clark, 1975.

Bentley, Peter and Philip J. Hughes. *Australian Life and the Christian Faith: Facts and Figures*. Victoria: Christian Research Association, 1998.

Berger, Peter L. *The Desecularization of the World: Resurgent Religion and World Politics*. Grand Rapids: Eerdmans Publishing, 1999.

Borg, Marcus. *The Heart of Christianity: Rediscovering a Life of Faith*. San Francisco: HarperCollins, 2004.

Bowden, John ed. *Thirty Years of Honesty, Honest to God: Then and Now*. London: SCM Press, 1993.

Bowker, John. *Licensed Insanities: Religions and Belief in God in the Contemporary World*. London: Darton, Longman and Todd, 1977.

Bruce, Steve. *God is Dead: Secularization in the West*. Oxford: Blackwell, 2002.

Carrette, Jeremy and Richard King. *Selling Spirituality: The Silent Takeover of Religion*. Oxford: Routledge, 2005.

Charlesworth, Max ed. *Religious Business: Essays on Aboriginal Spirituality*. Cambridge: CUP, 1998.

Collins, Paul. *God's Earth: Religion As if It Really Mattered*. Victoria: HarperCollins, 1995.

Cupitt, Don. *Taking Leave of God*. London: SCM Press, 1980.

————. *Radicals and the Future of the Church*. London: SCM Press, 1989.

————. *The Sea of Faith*. 2nd edition. London: BBC SCM Press, 1994.

————. *Kingdom Come in Everyday Speech*. London: SCM Press, 2000.

————. *The Revelation of Being*. London: SCM Press, 1998.

————. *Philosophy's Own Religion*. London: SCM Press, 2000.

————. "Christianity after the Church." Paper presented at UK Sea of Faith conference 2000.

————. *Reforming Christianity*. Santa Rosa: Polebridge Press, 2001.

————. *Emptiness and Brightness*. Santa Rosa: Polebridge Press, 2001.

Dawkins, Richard. "Snake Oil and Holy Water." *Forbes* (10 April 1999): 1–2.

D'Costa, Gavin. *Theology and Religious Pluralism: The Challenge of Other Religions*. Oxford: Blackwell, 1986.

Donovan, Vincent J. *Christianity Rediscovered: An Epistle from the Masai*. London: SCM Press, 1982.

Edwards, David L. *Tradition and Truth: The Challenge of England's Radical Theologians 1962–1989*. London: Hodder and Stoughton, 1989.

Flew, Antony. *God and Philosophy*. London: Hutchinson, 1966.

Forman, Robert K. C. *Grassroots Spirituality: What It Is, Why It Is Here, Where It Is Going*. Charlottesville: Imprint Academic, 2004.

Fraser, Giles. *Redeeming Nietzsche: On the Piety of Unbelief*. London: Routledge, 2002.

Freeman, Anthony. *God in Us: A Case for Christian Humanism*. London: SCM Press, 1993.

Funk, Robert. *Honest to Jesus: Jesus for a New Millennium*. San Francisco: HarperSanFrancisco, 1996.

——. ed. *The Once and Future Jesus*. Santa Rosa: Polebridge Press, 2000.

——. ed. *The Once and Future Faith*. Santa Rosa: Polebridge Press, 2001.

——. *A Credible Jesus: Fragments of a Vision*. Santa Rosa: Polebridge Press, 2002.

Geering, Lloyd. *The World to Come: From Christian Past to Global Future*. Santa Rosa: Polebridge Press, 1999

——. *Tomorrow's God: How We Create Our Worlds*. Santa Rosa: Polebridge Press, 2000.

——. *Christianity without God*. Santa Rosa: Polebridge Press, 2002.

——. *Fundamentalism: The Challenge to the Secular World*. Victoria: St. Andrew's Trust for the Study of Religion and Society, 2003.

——. *The Greening of Christianity*. Victoria: St. Andrew's Trust for the Study of Religion and Society, 2005.

Goodenough, Ursula. "What Science Can and Cannot Offer to a Religious Narrative." *Zygon: Journal of Religion and Science* 29, no. 3. (September 1994): 321–30.

——. "The Religious Dimensions of the Biological Narrative." *Zygon: Journal of Religion and Science* 29, no. 4 (December 1994): 603–18.

——. "There are two flavors of God people." http://beliefnet.com/story/147/story_14706.html.

——. *The Sacred Depths of Nature*. Oxford: Oxford University Press, 1998.

Gould, Stephen Jay. *Rocks of Ages: Science and Religion in the Fullness of Life*. New York: The Ballantine Publishing Group, 1999.

Goulder, Michael and John Hick. *Why believe in God?* London: SCM Press, 1983.

Harris, Sam. *The End of Faith: Religion, Terror and the Future of Reason*. London: The Free Press, 2005.

——. "An Atheist Manifesto." Available online: http://www.truthdig.com/dig/item/200512_an_atheist_manifesto.html.

Heelas, Paul and Linda Woodhead. *The Spiritual Revolution: Why Religion Is Giving Way to Spirituality*. Oxford: Blackwell, 2005.

Holloway, Richard. *Doubts and Loves: What Is Left of Christianity?* Edinburgh: Canongate, 2001.

———. *Looking in the Distance: The Human Search for Meaning.* Edinburgh: Canongate, 2005.

Howard, Anthony. *Basil Hume: The Monk Cardinal.* London: Headline, 2005.

Huntingdon, Samuel P. *The Clash of Civilizations and the Remaking of World Order.* New York: Simon and Schuster, 1996.

Jenks, Greg. *Faithfutures Guide No. 2.* Kenmore: Faithfutures, 2001.

Jones, Robert. *God, Galileo and Geering: A Faith for the 21st Century.* Santa Rosa: Polebridge Press, 2005.

Leaves, Nigel. *Odyssey on the Sea of Faith: The Life and Writings of Don Cupitt.* Santa Rosa: Polebridge Press, 2004.

———. *Surfing on the Sea of Faith: The Ethics and Religion of Don Cupitt.* Santa Rosa: Polebridge Press, 2005.

Lewis, C. S. *Mere Christianity.* San Francisco: HarperSanFrancisco, 2001.

Malouf, David. *An Imaginary Life.* New York: Braziller, 1978.

———. *A Spirit of Play: The Making of Australian Consciousness.* Sydney: ABC Books, 1998.

Manji, Irshad. *The Trouble with Islam Today: A Muslim's Call for the Reform in her Faith.* New York: St Martin's Press, 2005.

———. "When denial can kill; why we Muslims must admit that our religion might be motivating the bombers." *Time Magazine* (July 17, 2005).

McCourt Frank, *Angela's Ashes: A Memoir of a Childhood.* London: Flamingo, 1997.

McGillion, Chris. *The Chosen Ones.* Sydney: Allen and Unwin, 2005.

Midgley, Carol. "Spirited away: why the end is nigh for religion." *The Times* (November 4, 2004).

Nasrin, Taslima. *Shame.* New York: Prometheus Books, 1997.

———. *Meyebela: My Bengali Childhood: A Memoir of Growing Up Female in a Muslim World.* Vermont: Steerforth Press, 1998.

Nietzsche, Friedrich. *The Joyous Science.* London: Weidenfeld and Nicolson, 1965.

———. *Twilight of the Idols* and *The Anti-Christ.* London: Penguin, 1990.

Paterson, Torquil. "Why I resigned." Unpublished paper.

Pederby, Max. *Third World Conundrum: A Call to Christian Partnership.* Exeter: Paternoster Press, 1968.

Raiter, Michael. *Stirrings of the Soul.* Kingsford: Matthias Media, 2003.

Richter, Philip and Leslie Francis. *Gone but not Forgotten.* London: Darton, Longman & Todd, 1998.

Robbins, J. Wesley. "When Christians Become Naturalists." *Religious Studies* 28 (1992): 195–206.

Russell, Bertrand. *Why I Am Not a Christian.* London; Allen and Unwin, 1967.

Ruthven, Malise. *The Divine Supermarket: Shopping for God in America.* New York: Morrow, 1990.

Smuts, Barbara. "Sanctifying the Cosmos." *Scientific American* (May 1999). Available online: http://www.sciam.com/1999/0599issue/0599reviews1.html.

Spearritt, Greg. "Religion: It's Natural!" *Sea of Faith in Australia Bulletin* (May 2003).

———. *Fundamentalism: The Search for Meaning.* Oxford: Oxford University Press, 2005.

Spong, John Shelby. *Why Christianity Must Change or Die: A Bishop Speaks to Believers in Exile.* San Francisco: HarperSanFrancisco, 1998.

———. *Here I Stand: My Struggle for a Christianity of Integrity, Love and Equality.* San Francisco: HarperSanFrancisco, 2000.

———. *A New Christianity for a New World: Why Traditional Faith is Dying and How a New Faith is Being Born.* San Francisco: HarperSanFrancisco, 2001.

———. *The Sins of Scripture: Exposing the Bible's Texts of Hate to Reveal the God of Love.* San Francisco: HarperSanFrancisco, 2005.

Stacey, Nicholas. *Who Cares?* London: Blond, 1971.

Sutcliffe, Steven and Marion Bowman eds. *Beyond New Age: Exploring Alternative Spirituality.* Edinburgh: Edinburgh University Press, 2000.

Swinburne, Richard. *The Existence of God.* Oxford: Oxford University Press, 1979.

Tacey, David. *ReEnchantment: The New Australian Spirituality.* Sydney: Harper Collins, 2000.

Taussig, Hal. *A New Spiritual Home: Progressive Christianity at the Grass Roots.* Santa Rosa, Polebridge Press, 2006.

Thomas, Lewis. *The Lives of a Cell: Notes of a Biology Watcher.* New York: Penguin, 1978.

Victorin-Vangerud, Nancy M. "The Sacred Edge: Seascape as Spiritual Resource for an Australian Eco-eschatology." *Ecotheology* 6.2 (2001): 167–85.

Waldman, Steven ed. *From the Ashes: A Spiritual Response to the Attack on America.* USA: Rodale and Beliefnet, 2001.

Webb, Stephen H. Review of *The Sacred Depths of Nature* by Ursula Goodenough, *Reviews in Religion and Theology* 7, no. 2 (2000): 237.

Winton, Tim. *The Land's Edge.* Sydney: Picador, 1993.

# INDEX

**Nigel Leaves** is Warden and Dean of Studies of John Wollaston Anglican Theological College, Perth, Western Australia. An Anglican priest who served in Papua New Guinea, Hong Kong and Australia, he is the author of *Odyssey on the Sea of Faith: the life and writings of Don Cupitt* (2004) and *Surfing on the Sea of Faith: the religion and ethics of Don Cupitt* (2005).